Safari, according to the "Encarta Dictionary" is defined as "a journey across a piece of land, especially in Africa." To that I would add "a journey and experiences that magically transforms the heart and mind of the participant so that the desire to do it all over again is never far from their thoughts. Let me share with you a little taste of the African twilight.

When I get back to camp and the days hunt is over is my favorite time on safari. It is the magical time of the African sunset. Do not get me wrong the sunrises can be spectacular but I love the sunsets. Let me take you there with me; try to imagine yourself there as I describe the evening. The sky turns the most wonderful shades of blue, and the shadows seem to move across the ground on their own. The temperature drops quickly and you shiver while you change from your hunting clothes into your camp attire. Next, you catch that first smell of smoke coming off the fire and it draws you closer to the only source of heat. Waiting close to the fire is your host with your favorite beverage. A "sundowner" is what the locals call it. It is more than just having a drink; it is about winding up the day and winding you down. You pull your chair up to the fire, enjoy a smoke if you like, and lots of great conversation. If there is more than one hunter in your group, you can relive each other's adventures of the day. Old stories are retold and all becomes right with the world, or at least this little corner of it. As the story swapping comes to an end, and the liquid from you last refill works its way toward the bottom of your glass, your nose may catch a whiff of the delights to come. A few minutes later the call will come to assemble for dinner, and as you make your way toward the table, your senses are completely overwhelmed. Here in the deepest, darkest, Africa is a table set with fine china and crystal. There are decanters of fine wine, bowls of steaming vegetables, and a platter of roasted beast. The sight forces you to concentrate on not drooling down your shirt and embarrassing yourself. As you look around the table, you realize that you are not alone in your plight, as everyone in attendance seems to be having the same problem. When everyone is seated, a short blessing is asked, and the feast begins. The conversation magically ceases for the first few minutes of dinner as everyone enjoys each bite. Just as finally convince your mouth to stop taking in any more food, your sense of smell is assaulted once more by what else, desert. Pastries, pies, puddings, or cake, what would it be tonight? All of this food will ruin even the most staunch dieters resolve. After everyone has had to loosen his or her belt a notch or two, it is back to the fire with one last glass of wine. For those that enjoy a good cigar, I cannot think of a better time or place to enjoy a smoke. The conversation soon turns to coming up with a game plan for tomorrow and then to which quarry you are searching. Once again, the conversation starts to lag. Others start to excuse themselves and head off to bed and you fight the urge to follow. There is something about sitting around the fire watching the fames dance while enjoying the serenade provided courtesy of the African night. It is easy to think back fifty or a hundred years and imagine what it was like then. It was probably not too much different from what you are experiencing tonight. You wonder what the hunters that came before you talked about. Were they hunting elephant, lion, plains game, or the same as you? Soon the realization that you cannot resist the call of your warm comfortable bed any longer works its way into your conscious thought. As you stand and force one foot in front and head toward your quarters you feel the cold of the night wrap its self around you. You are barely able to get your things ready for tomorrow as sleep comes for you. As you drift off, a thought comes to you and you smile as you realize that you get to do this all again tomorrow.

Safari 101

HUNTING AFRICA: *THE ULTIMATE ADVENTURE*

Getting There
AND BACK

David L. Brown

NEW YORK

Safari 101

HUNTING AFRICA:*THE ULTIMATE ADVENTURE*
Getting There AND BACK
David L. Brown

ISBN 978-1-61448-142-3 Paperback
ISBN 978-1-61448-143-0 eBook

Published by:
MORGAN JAMES PUBLISHING
The Entrepreneurial Publisher
5 Penn Plaza, 23rd Floor
New York City, New York 10001
(212) 655-5470 Office
(516) 908-4496 Fax
www.MorganJamesPublishing.com

Cover Design by:
Rachel Lopez
rachel@r2cdesign.com

Interior Design by:
Bonnie Bushman
bbushman@bresnan.net

In an effort to support local communities, raise awareness and funds, Morgan James Publishing donates a percent of all book sales for the life of each book to Habitat for Humanity Peninsula and Greater Williamsburg.
Get involved today, visit
www.HelpHabitatForHumanity.org.

Dedication

I would like to express my gratitude to my wife for her momentary lapse in sanity when she allowed me to go on my first safari and get me started on a lifelong love affair with the Dark Continent. I also want to say how blessed I am to have a wife that allows my passion for hunting Africa to continue and for encouraging me to put my thoughts on paper

I want to say a big thank you to Sally Frye for all of the hard work she put in proofreading and editing Safari 101. Without her, Safari 101 would still be just a jumble of thoughts stored in a computer file.

I would like to thank Rick Wilks for doing such a fantastic job in matching me up with my Processional Hunters; Johann Veldsman and Phillip Smyth. I also have to say thank you to Johann for his ability to teach me without me realizing I was being taught and being the principal reason that I was bitten by the safari bug. Thank you, Phillip, for introducing me to the adrenalin-filled lifestyle called dangerous game hunting.

Thank you to CZ USA for building me three of the finest rifles I have ever owned.

Thanks to Gracy Travel for getting me back and forth across the Atlantic so many times without a single hiccup.

Finally, I want to thank all the good folks at Morgan James Publishing. You have all put up with my dumb questions and shown me the utmost patience.

Table of Contents

Safari 101

Safari. The mention of the word conjures excitement, mystery, and a sense of, "I always wanted to do that". In the chapters that follow, I will whet your appetite, give you some helpful hints, so instead of having to say "I always wanted to do that", you can say "I did that."

CHAPTER ONE
My Start

The desire to go on safari most often starts as a little ember in the back of your mind. If that is the case, you have plenty of time to do your research and plan everything thoroughly. The way I started was with the local hunting and fishing trade show. I was looking at the new hunting and fishing gear when I found myself standing in front of a booth that said "Wilks' Safari Adventures". Standing there talking with Rick, that little ember in the back of my mind started to grow and become a small flame. He showed me photos of the animals that were available and told me which country offered each animal. The varieties of species and types of hunts that were available were too numerous for me to comprehend. The prices of the safaris were all reasonable and, more often than not, they were about two thirds of a fully guided hunt in the Western United States. The cost, however, was still more than I could afford at the time, so I left with a brochure and a business card that listed his web address. When I got home from the show, the first thing I did was to look up Rick's website and bookmark it for future reference. I did not know exactly when I would need the website, only that I would need it sometime in the future. I really wanted that sometime to be sooner than later.

About three years down the road, a bit of bad luck actually turned into good luck and sent me to Africa for the first time. A friend of mine that had grown in up in Wyoming decided he wanted to return to his roots, go back there, and do some hunting. I was ecstatic when he asked me if I want to go along. Now all I had to do was get permission from my wife. For the most part, she is not overly fond of my hunting activities, and at times I am sure that she just barely tolerates them. Normally, when I ask to go on one of my "adventures", her eyes sort of glaze over and she looks at me like I have horns growing out the side of my head and am speaking gibberish. Armed with that knowledge and prior experience, it was obvious I had my work cut out for me. Some serious scheming and contemplating led me to the conclusion that, if the circumstances were just right, I could get her permission. My main reasoning would be that this was going to be an inexpensive hunting trip. We would be hunting on family land with his brother as a guide, so the cost would be more reasonable. Additionally, if we drove, instead of flying, the cost of the trip would then be an exceptional bargain. My logic was: would any woman be able to pass up such a bargain? When I explained this to my wife, it only took a little begging and a few tears to secure her permission. With permission granted, my friend and I quickly filled out the required paperwork to enter the lottery for a Wyoming hunting license. The next few months were wonderful. By day, we planned our trip; and, at night, we dreamt about hunting under the vast western skies. There was a lot to keep us busy while we anxiously waited for our Wyoming hunting licenses. When the letter finally came, I tore into it and could not believe it when I read the first six words. "We are sorry to inform you," it said, "but your party was not selected to receive hunting tags for this year. Please try again next year." I had gone from ecstatic to dejected in about two seconds. This was supposed to be my first big hunting trip. What was I going to do now? I frantically tried to come up with a new plan. After all, my wife had given me permission to go on a trip, but now I had nowhere to go. Then it happened. That little ember, still glowing from years ago, burst into flame. Africa was the answer to my dilemma.

With a quick trip to my computer, I checked Rick's website. Yes, it was still there. I quickly found his phone number and gave him a call. I explained what happened to me and asked if he had any openings. He said possibly, but we would need to talk a little bit first. For the next 30 to 45 minutes, he asked me questions, some more questions, and even more questions. I did not understand why he needed to know so much about me, but I answered all of them anyway. When the marathon question session was over, Rick had to do some checking before he could get back to me with an answer. As soon as I hung up, it dawned on me that I had one more hurdle to clear; I had to get this idea past my wife. I sat there for a few minutes trying to come up with some logical explanation of how Wyoming turned into Africa, but I was too excited to think clearly. When I could not think of anything to tell her, I did what every good husband would do. I decided to put it off until I had more information. The next three days were unbearable. Would he be able to find something? Was it too late in the season? What if he could not find anything? The more I thought about it, the more I drove myself nuts.

By the time the phone finally rang, I had convinced myself of the worst. My first trip was over before it even started. When Rick said, "Good news! I have got a spot for you!", my mind changed gears so quickly that I almost gave myself whiplash. All I could say was, "Great. When and where?" As Rick began to fill in the details, it started to sink in; I was going on my first Safari. He told me that I would be hunting with a PH (Professional Hunter) by the name of Johann Veldsman. Johann and his wife, Vera, had started "Shona Hunting Adventures" the previous year and still had openings available. When I expressed some concern over this being a new company, Rick assured me that I would have the time of my life, as he had hunted with Johann before. He said that Johann was the "real deal". When I asked him to explain, he told me that Johann's father was a geologist and that Johann had been raised in the bush all over Africa. Cool, I thought, the African version of a "mountain man". Next, he told me the details. I was to arrive the first day of August 2006, hunt the 2nd through the 9th, and depart on the 10th. I would be in Namibia on a "plains game package". The package would include a Kudu, a Gemsbok, a Warthog and a Duiker or Steinbuck. It would also include airport transfers, room and board, licenses, and just about everything but tips. Best of all, the entire package was only $3500.00 U.S. He also gave me some contact information on the people he used to book his personal travel to Africa. He left it up to me whether to call them or not, but he recommended them. Lastly, he told me that as soon as he received my deposit, he would send me a packet of information, and if I had any questions not to hesitate to call or e-mail him.

The African Version of a Mountian Man, Johann Veldsman

I was apprehensive about approaching my wife with the idea of going to Africa. She was not too crazy about me traveling inside the United States. What would she say about going far, far away, or the extra cost? Much to my relief, she saw how enthusiastic I was, and consented to me going on my dream hunt. She did tell me that she wanted a special vacation the following year and, without really thinking, I immediately agreed. I was going on Safari! That was the start of a love affair with Africa. I returned to Africa numerous times since my first Safari and even took my wife and children on a Safari of their own. It was just dumb luck that I found the right combination of people to help me with my first Safari. I will share what I have learned with you, make things a little less stressful and a lot more fun, and gently turn that little ember in the back of your mind into a small flame.

CHAPTER TWO

Fanning the Ember: Why Go on Safari?

The first reason to go on a safari in Africa is just because it is Africa. Most Americans have a distorted vision of Africa. We have no actual experience with the continent or just a limited view from a few people that we happen to know. We Americans get way too much of our perspective from television. We either see a "paradise" disrupted by the evil white hunter as in the "Tarzan" movies, or the poor starving children in the charity commercials. We see the political unrest in some of the countries on the six o'clock news. We see an AIDS epidemic and natural disasters. What we do not see are a group of all races who, for the most part, are working very hard to make a living for themselves and improvements for the future. We do not see the success stories like wildlife management that have brought several species of animals from threatened to population levels that are beyond carrying capacity. We do not see the modern cities with modern medical centers, or a standard of living much like our own. All of these are Africa, all rolled up into a magical and mystical place, a place where the wild things roam, a place for the visit of a lifetime.

Africa is a hunter's paradise. The number of species and quantity of animals boggles the mind of most American hunters. We are used to going after one big game species at a time, with most of us having only a remote possibility of running into another big game species during the same hunt. You can never be sure what you are going to run into

when you venture into the African bush. You might be looking for a kudu but run into a record book gemsbok. If you are looking for a cape buffalo, keep an eye out for elephants or lions. It all depends on where you are. If you have booked a package hunt, you can take three, six, or even more animals. Large animals or small animals, your only limitation is the amount of time you have and your pocket book. Plains game such as the Kudu, gemsbok, eland, impala,

Author with 1st African Trophy a Gold Medal Steinbuck

wildebeest, and springbok are just a few of the larger species of antelope that are available. If you would like something smaller, consider taking one of the "Tiny Ten", The African Grand Slam of mini antelope. Have you ever heard of the klipspringer, dik-dik, duiker, or steinbuck? They are just a few members of "the Ten". These small antelope start at about fifteen pounds and are amazingly tough to hunt. If that does not do it for you, how about hunting the aquatic animals, like the hippopotamus or Nile crocodile? While you are hunting these, you could take an afternoon off and enjoy the fantastic fishing available in some locations. Still not sold? Avid bird hunters

The Kudu demonstraiting his ability to disapear in the blink of an eye

have a chance to put their wing shooting skills to use as well. Sand grouse, doves, and guinea fowl are just a sample of the fantastic wing shooting that Africa has to offer.

Two of the best tellers of African tales, Robert Ruark and Peter Capstick were both extremely fond wing shooting. After reading their accounts of bird hunting, I wanted to experience it for myself. On my first trip, I had taken my Kudu during a morning hunt and, on the way back, Johann asked me if I wanted to bird hunt that afternoon. When I responded with an enthusiastic, "Yes!", he asked me another question. "Do you want the hunt the way you Americans hunt, or the way we learned as kids here in Africa?" I knew it was a baited question but I rose to the challenge and answered, "The way you did it as a kid." After lunch and with my answer in mind, he headed to the gun locker in preparation for our afternoon hunt. Instead of returning with a shotgun as I expected, he came back with a 22 rimfire. Even though I consider myself a better-than-average wing shot, I told him he could not possibly expect me to hit a flying bird with a 22. He explained that we would shoot them on the ground as they ran from the truck. It did not seem sporting to me to shoot the large bird while it was on the ground, even if I was using a 22, and I told him this. His reply was that "only head shots count". He got quite a few laughs from me trying to hit a head that was bobbing from side to side like a metronome turned all the way up. He finally took mercy on me and explained that, instead of trying to lead the bobbing head, I should try to time my shot to intercept the head on the return swing. With that advice, I connected

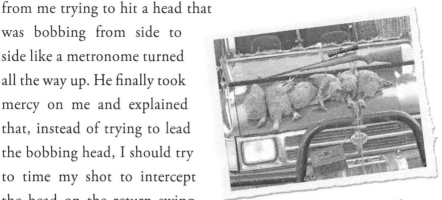

Guinea Fowl With a .22

on my next shot and then made the mistake of saying, "This isn't so hard". It took me another fifteen shots before I hit another bird. We had a wonderful afternoon of shooting and bagged enough birds to feed the staff and ourselves that night. It was a few years later when I got to try some actual wing shooting. My new friend and PH, Phillip Smythe, was kind enough to loan me his Greener 12 gauge so I could attempt to bag a few sand grouse. You will notice I said, "attempt" to bag a few sand grouse. Those rascals fly like doves with full afterburners! Since the best time to hunt them is at dusk, it is difficult shooting at best. I finally took a few and we had the breast meat wrapped in bacon that night for appetizers. We cooked them over the fire and enjoyed them with a glass of South African wine.

After you have some plains game experience, and want to up the adrenalin factor, consider one of the "Big Five". The African grand slam consists of the lion, leopard, Cape buffalo, elephant, and rhino. When you hunt these "Dangerous Game" (or DG) animals, something that is always on your mind is knowing that any one of these animals could kill or severely injure you. These animals will stomp, bite, eat, or gore you, if given half a chance, and are very capable of doing so.

Authors Cape Buffalo and 416 Rigby

That being said, a dangerous game hunt is an experience like no other. On my second dangerous game hunt, I was after Cape buffalo. On that hunt, there was a group of young lions after the same buffalo that we were. While we only saw them from a distance, knowing that we could run into the lions at any time was never far from my thoughts. We also met up with a group of park rangers just minutes after they captured a group of poachers. These poachers were just a few hundred yards away from where we were hunting and that experience was quite unnerving. I do not know if these poachers were armed or not, but I do know that I like my encounters with dangerous things in the African bush to be with the four-legged kind, not with the two-legged variety. Elephants were also a concern, as we continually had to dodge them trying to get to the buffalo. It might sound like too much for some, but I am hooked and cannot wait to do it all again. If stalking is not your game, you can hunt leopard over bait from a blind. If sitting in a blind does not sound too exciting, just remember as you walk out in the pitch black of an African night, that the leopard can see in the dark much better than you can and that he is close. If he were not close, your PH would not have put a blind there.

You will never feel as alive as you do on a DG hunt. The Big Five are not the only dangerous animals to hunt in Africa; some antelope can be dangerous as well. Two types of antelope in particular, the sable and gemsbok, account for more than a few injuries and even a few deaths each year. **Never** approach a downed antelope from the front. If it is not dead and tries to get up, it will drop its head to help it stand, and, as it regains its feet, the head and horns thrust upward and forward. Trust me, you do not want to be in front of the animal if this happens.

One last type of hunt that would fall into the adrenalin category is a problem animal hunt. Unless you have the means to drop everything and fly to Africa, you will probably have to be in the right spot at the right time to get one of these hunts. A problem animal is normally a dangerous game animal that has killed someone, or caused property damage on multiple occasions. When this happens, the local authorities will often call local PHs to come and dispose of the animal. If the PH feels his hunter is up to the task they will go and hunt the animal. A trophy fee is required but is normally only a fraction of the normal cost. The proceeds most likely will go to compensate the victim's family or to pay for damages. To me, this is the ultimate thrill hunt. You are hunting an animal that has lost its fear of man and may be hunting you. On my last trip to Namibia, Johann got a call about an elephant that killed a farm worker in a nearby community. It was just my bad luck that another PH was able to get there quicker and I missed the opportunity. In addition to getting to hunt the animal, you are also doing the community a huge favor. All of the meat goes to feed the local community. Some years ago, one of my friends had the opportunity to take a problem elephant. He had some moral trepidations about hunting elephant, but the fact it was a problem animal changed his mind. The hunt and celebration that followed were captured on video. I will never forget one scene. Part of the meat from the elephant went to the local orphanage and Claude went along for the delivery. It was the only meat at the orphanage would get for some time. When the children found out what was going on, they ran out of the school and started a song of thanks to Claude. All of the emotion of the hunt and the joy of the children were more than he could stand and the tears flowed. This, my friend, is a success story for everyone involved. Normally, during a problem animal hunt, the hunter gets to keep nothing. Fortunately, the governments of some countries are thinking about letting the hunter keep the trophy parts of the animal taken. I think this is only fair since you are paying a fee. Even if you do not get anything but pictures, you have an incredible experience and a great story to share.

One small footnote about dangerous critters in Africa: keep your eyes open for snakes and scorpions. Even though most of the hunting is done in the winter months, snakes can still be a problem during this season in Africa. A great many of the snakes have particularly nasty venom. There are Mambas, cobras, puff adders and gaboon vipers to mention a few. If you follow my Boy Scouts' first rule of hiking, you should not have a problem. That rule is to never step over something on the trail, but, instead, to step on it, look down, and then step off. If you follow this advice, you will considerably reduce your odds of stepping on a snake. Scorpions are not really a problem, but I always shake out my boots before putting them on.

Hunters make a huge economic impact in Africa. Anti-hunters will tell you that the eco or photo safaris do as much good, but I disagree. I would like to give you some information and let you make up your own mind, and perhaps give you enough information to change the minds of a few others as well. While it is true that both a hunter and eco tourist pay a daily rate and are responsible for the employment of housekeeping staff, cooks and a guide, that is where the similarities end. A lot of the eco-tourist money goes to the government of whatever national park in which they happen to be. The hunter's money can go to the private landowner as well; it does not have to trickle down to get into the people's hands. The hunter will also leave money in trophy fees. These trophy fees can go toward a multitude of things. The portion going to the landowner, either public or private gives the landowner incentive to manage land for the betterment of wild game. They can add waterholes and leave land undeveloped. It reimburses landowners for any damage done by game species, such as broken fences or damaged crops. Another portion goes directly to the government. The money trains rangers and anti-poaching units. Speaking of poaching, every day that the PH and his clients are in the bush, it is a "boots on the ground" poaching deterrent. Not that they actually fight poachers, but I have found and removed snares, and one of the PHs I was with reported the signs of poaching we encountered back to the authorities. This report led to the eventual arrest of several poachers. The money also gives the government reason to listen to biologists and PHs, not politicians, when it comes to quotas for game management purposes. It also gives the governments incentive to make coming and going as easy as possible for hunters. The more hunter-friendly a country is, the more hunters that country will attract, and that means more money spent. There are even a few African countries that would have little to no foreign income without the fees from hunters. In addition to the staff mentioned above, hunters are responsible for the employment of trackers, skinners, butchers, taxidermists, and apprentice PHs. They indirectly employ shipping companies when they ship the trophies back home. In my estimation, hunters spend two to three times what an eco-tourist spends.

There is a huge protein shortage in many African countries and the hunter helps here as well. Virtually no part of a game animal goes unused. The hunting camp will use only part of the meat from the game harvested as food for clients and staff rations. Depending on where you are, the rest either is given to a local village or taken to a local butcher shop and sold at very reasonable prices. In a good year, a hunting camp could supply thousands of pounds of inexpensive protein to the local population. The indigenous people even consume the internal organs, as delicacies. The hides that are not required for taxidermy work are often sold to local artisans for a nominal fee. In the artisans' hands, these skins become items for sale to the general population and to tourists. Some larger companies will also use the hides from locally harvested game. The Courteney Boot Company in Zimbabwe makes an excellent boot from buffalo and impala skins. I own a pair and they are wonderful. Not having to pay a lot for leather helps keep the company profitable and people employed.

The most important thing that the hunting safari industry does is conservation. How does hunting and killing an animal conserve an animal? It is very simple once you stop and think about it. It gives a game animal value. Giving an animal a cash value makes it worth saving. Which would be taken better care of, "Item A" with a value of $10.00, the price a poacher would get for bush meat, or "Item B" worth $1000.00 to a trophy hunter? Obviously "B" would be taken better care of than "A". It works the same way with animals; the more value it has, the better the care it is given. A farmer will put up with some crop damage by wildlife, if a hunter pays him for the privilege of hunting the wildlife on his farm. A rancher will put up with a leopard or lion if a hunter will pay him to be able to come and hunt it. It has even become so profitable that some ranchers and farmers now manage for game animals as much as they do for crops or cattle. What happens if an animal has no value? Let me tell you about the cheetah. I learned on my first trip to Namibia that the local ranchers called the cheetah a shoot-and-shovel animal. When I asked what that meant, the answer I was given has caused me great angst ever since. When a rancher sees a cheetah, he shoots it, takes his shovel, and buries it on the spot. At the time, I thought that the cheetah was protected by the CITES (Convention on International Trade in Endangered Species) treaty. In fact, the CITES treaty only prohibits the international trade of animal products of the species on its list. The fact that hunters cannot take a cheetah trophy home makes it an undesirable animal to hunt. Since Namibia has a very healthy population of the cats and no one wants to hunt the animals, thus taking away its value, the ranchers are handling the predatory animals the only way they can. To me, it is somewhat sad that a treaty to protect animals is in fact doing them harm.

The Okavango Delta of Botswana has been a hunter's paradise. Through the combination of smart game management and hunters' dollars, there are fantastic quantities of game. The elephant population is currently about 2 to 2-1/2 times its carrying capacity. There are also healthy populations of Cape buffalo, lions, and many species of plains game. Did you notice that I said, "Has been"? Currently, there is a possibility the government of Botswana will move away from the hunting tourism and its success, toward the eco tourist. If this happens, the Okavango Delta will become the biggest wildlife experiment that ever happened. By "experiment," I mean we will be able to be see if the eco dollar and its supporters can take as good care of this world treasure as the hunters have who are currently taking care of it. Another troublesome possibility is what happens to the unarmed eco tourist when they accidentally take photos that armed poachers do not want taken. I have two fears about this situation. I am afraid for hunters if the eco-tourism movement succeeds and actually takes care of the animal population. I am more afraid for the animals if the eco-tourism movement succeeds and is not able to take care of the animals. Time will tell.

CHAPTER THREE
Choose Your Team

L et us start with a few definitions to avoid confusion down the road. The first is "Booking Agent", this person or company will help you select your Safari Operator or your PH. It should cost you nothing to use a booking agent because their pay comes in the form of a commission from the Safari Operator. The Safari Operator is an individual that often has several hunting areas and PHs that they work for. A PH is your guide and mentor in the field while you are hunting. A Safari Operator and PH can be, but are not necessarily one in the same. With the risk of offending the women in the trade, I will refer to all of the above in the masculine form, so I can keep things simple.

Hint number one: When you start investigating the possibility of booking a Safari, get a notebook and keep it forever. Keep notes on everything. For each step, item, or section, write down the date, who you talked to, and then the subject of the conversation. Keep a list of any questions that may come up so you cannot forget to ask them later. This will be your safari bible. If there is a discrepancy in the trip details, you can go back to your notes and say, "I talked to such and such on a certain day, date, and time." You will be surprised just how often you can settle a disagreement before it even gets started. When you start a new topic, draw a horizontal line across the page to indicate the different topics. When you complete the task in a section, draw a large "X" through the section when you complete it. By just drawing an "X", you can go back and still read things if you need to.

How do you select or find a Booking Agent? A good place to find one is at your local hunting and fishing trade show. If that does not pan out, ask around at your local gun shop or gun/hunt club. I have never run into anyone that has hunted Africa who was not more than willing to share his or her experience and knowledge. Lastly, look on line. It will take some sorting through, but there are a lot of names out there to choose from. Personally, I like the idea of meeting them face-to-face. That gives you a chance to get to know them a little. Best-case scenario is that there will be a good first impression, and the two of you will take a liking to each other. If you do not, I would keep looking. You will be spending a lot of time on the phone and e-mailing each other, so a good relationship is critical. He will probably have a website, so visit it often. It will give you an idea of the types of game, hunting camps, and locations that he represents. Take notes and ask questions when you talk to him. **Hint number two: check the website over time to make sure it is updated with new pictures, price list and maybe even new camps or locations.** Someone that is really in the business will keep his website updated. If they do not, it can cause them problems and aggravate potential clients. Imagine trying to book a trip only to find that the price is two years old, or that the local government has cut the quota of an animal that you want to take and it is no longer available. Be upfront with your booking agent. Let him know if you prefer a particular species and country, and if you would like any side trips. Side trips could be to a national park, a fishing trip or other sightseeing. If you have a budget, let him know that as well. Your booking agent should then ask you a boatload of questions. He should ask what kind of shape you are in, what type of hunting you like to do, if you are interested in a package hunt, when you want to go, and on and on. The more he knows about you, the better job he can do matching you with a hunt and a PH. A lot of questions might not sound that important, but they are. In my case, Rick did a great job of matching me with a PH. Johann and I met as strangers; we parted as hunting buddies. We like to hunt the same way, have the same philosophy on hunting, love old guns and calibers, have the same sense of humor, and the list goes on and on. I cannot imagine being on the continent and not stopping in for a hunt or visit. It goes without saying that my hunt was fantastic.

I want to give you a few questions to ask your booking agent. Ask him if he has been to where he is trying to send you, and if he has hunted with your PH. It is always best if he has firsthand knowledge of the hunt you are going on. It gives him the inside scoop on your PH's hunting style, his success rate, the type of terrain and the quality of the camp. If he has been there and done that, he can describe things with 100 percent certainty and give you an exact picture of what you will encounter. I am not saying do not go if he has not been there himself, but I am saying that you are relying on hearsay not knowledge. Ask him how long he has been in business. The longer he has been booking hunts for clients, the more likely it is that he has most of the bugs worked out of the system. Ask him for references, both good and, if he will give them, bad. While it is nice to know all the good things, it is more important to know if anything went wrong. If you discover any problems, get both sides of the story. Then you will know if it was "sour grapes" or a real problem. If you think the problem is real, ask what he did to correct it and prevent future occurrences.

Your booking agent should be able to talk knowledgably about all aspects of the hunt. If he is truly knowledgeable about taking a Safari, there will be countless comments and suggestions on things that have not even crossed your mind--little things like taking a pair of bed shoes for midnight trips to the bathroom, saline spray to keep your nose moist in the dry African climate, and so forth. This next statement might sound a little odd, but you want your booking agent to be a little opinionated. If all of the other pieces of the puzzle have fallen into place, trust his opinion about where you should go and what you should hunt. The more strongly he feels about something, the more you should listen to him. Remember, it is his job to make sure you have fun and a successful hunt. If he suggests a plains game hunt as a first Safari instead of a dangerous game hunt, listen to his reasons why. You could even use his reasons for a plains game hunt to be your first hunt as an excuse to your wife for a second hunt later on. If you can only go once and want to hunt dangerous game, tell him that and he should do his best to make it work. After he has all of the information, your booking agent will be able to suggest a Safari Company or PH for you. He may also suggest a hunting package or a daily rate with trophy fees. A package deal is normally the best and most economical way to go. A package should include: transfers from the airport, room and board, hunting license, or government permits, trophy fees, trophy preparation for the taxidermist, and just about everything but tips for your PH and his staff. If you do not take one of the trophies in your package, you will receive a refund of the trophy fee. A daily rate is a daily dollar amount that covers your room, board, and hunting expenses. Trophy fees, transfers, trophy prep, are all a la carte. Either way will give you a final cost. Once you have everything set and a final cost, you will have to send your booking agent a deposit to confirm your hunt. This is normally somewhere around one-half the cost of the hunt. You will pay the balance on the completion of the hunt. Be sure to ask your Safari Operator or PH if they want U.S. funds or travelers checks. If you do not want to carry that much cash with you, you may have a couple of other options. The first thing you could do is send another check to your booking agent and let him pay the bill for you. You would have to do this early enough for the check to clear before you leave. Some Safari Operators and PHs have offices in the United States and you can prepay there as well. The last option is to wire money directly to the Operator's or PH's Bank account overseas. If you choose to prepay, be sure to take a copy of the receipt with you just in case there is a paperwork screw-up somewhere down the line. When your booking agent receives your deposit, he will send you a deposit confirmation packet with helpful information and a list of suggested things to take. I will go into more detail about this later.

For my first trip, Rick suggested Johann Veldsman. He is the Safari Operator, PH and owner all rolled into one. Since he is all three, and to keep things simple, in this next section I will use the term PH for all three titles. When your booking agent suggests a PH, ask him why he feels the two of you are a good match. Listen carefully and make sure his logic makes sense to you. A few more questions to ask are: is the PH easy to work with, is he easily adaptable to your style and hunting abilities, and will you be the only one in camp or does he mix groups? If your PH cannot adapt to your abilities, you will likely come back disgruntled and empty-handed. You should also ask your PH (or booking agent, for that matter) what types of communications are available at camp. It will ease the minds of those you leave at home if you can let them know that you have arrived safely and that they can reach you in an emergency. While the camps have cell phones or radios, they are not set up to make international calls. In the camps I have been in, email has been the easiest, most consistent and reliable way to get messages in and out of camp.

Unless you are a real people person, I would not suggest having another group and PH in camp. Although almost all hunters get along in like company, there is a chance the other hunter did not do as much homework as you did and may not be having as much fun as you are. If that is true, his bad mood and sour attitude has a way of spreading to everyone in camp. The opposite could be just as true. Their positive attitude and outlook could rub off just as well. I would recommend knowing if it is a shared camp, so you can plan accordingly. Ask for the PH's contact information and, if he has a website, you can contact him with questions that you think of later. Most PHs will welcome your questions. It shows them your interest and allows them to get to know you before you arrive in camp. You and your PH should use any means to get to know each other before you get to camp. While you are in Africa, you are dependent on your PH. He will be your teacher and get you into position to take your animal.

Hint number three: listen to your PH as if your life depended on it, because it very well could. As I mentioned earlier, there are lots of things in Africa that bite, scratch or stomp. His knowledge is all that separates them from you. At the very least, listen, because you are paying him a lot of money to take a trophy animal and your success depends on him. Once you establish contact with your PH, it would not hurt to repeat some of the things you told your booking agent, such as your ability as a hunter, your physical condition, and your hunting style. Things sometimes get lost in translation and I consider this cheap insurance. It makes sure that neither one of you will have an unpleasant surprise when you finally meet. It will be an easy start of a dialogue between you and your PH. A simple dialogue can get the two of you comfortable with each other by asking and answering questions before you get to camp and it will give you a head start on things when you meet and start your hunt. I do not want to imply that you should flood your PH's inbox with hundreds of e-mails. He will have other clients to take care of and he will be in the bush a considerable amount of time. What I do suggest is to keep a small notepad with you at all times, even beside the bed at night. Use it to make a list of questions until you have a half dozen or so, then copy them to your "safari bible notepad. When you have your list, send him one e-mail with your questions. This will accomplish a few things. First, it will give you time to repeatedly think through your questions so they can be clear and concise. This way, you can put them into related groups and get you an answer correlated in a logical progression. Your list will also cut down on duplicate or similar questions. This will save your PH time and you will not sound like an unorganized newbie. As far as questions go, remember this: the only dumb question is the one that you do not ask. Do not get all the way to Africa and find out that you could have saved yourself a large headache if you had just asked a simple question. One last thing to remember about asking your PH questions: it will probably take some time for your PH to get back to you. He may be in the bush, busy with a client, or just plain tired.

Why have I emphasized opening a line of communication? Very simple, it is one of the easiest ways to make sure your trip goes the way you want it to and with as few bumps in the road as possible. Let me give you an example. It was not long after Rick got my deposit that Johann sent me an introductory e-mail with a few facts about "Shona Hunting Adventures", a suggested bring-with-you list, and a questionnaire (see appendices). The "what-to-bring list" had some different items than Rick's list, so I cross-referenced the two, but the questionnaire threw me. I could not figure it out until opened the attachment.

The questions it asked allowed Johann to custom fit the camp to me. He wanted to know everything from my age, to my hunting experience, to what kind of food and drink I liked, from medical problems to allergies, and more. When I got there, the camp was set up as much as possible to my needs and taste. It was as if I could have stepped in to a tent camp with Teddy Roosevelt or Robert Ruark; it was just as I had imagined it would be.

My first impression of camp was preceded by a delay at the airport with lost luggage and a four-hour drive. I was frustrated and disappointed by the lost baggage ordeal, but at least my guns had made it. When I finally made it to the reception area of the airport, my afternoon dramatically improved when Johann's wife Vera met me for my transfer to camp. She told me not to worry about my bag. It would probably only be "temporally" lost, and, when the airline found them, the bags would promptly be delivered to where they were supposed to be. She explained that Johann was held up helping out another PH and would arrive in camp early tomorrow morning in time to start my hunt. We soon had my gear loaded into the land cruiser, and off we went.

I learned many things in the next four hours as we headed north from the airport. By the time we got to camp, I felt as if I had known Vera for quite some time. I was to be hunting her family's farm and cattle ranch. It was small. According to her, it was only 12,500 acres, but I was not to worry as they had arrangements made with the surrounding farms and had worked up a small concession of 50,000 acres. I would hate to see her definition of large after seeing what she calls small. As the hours past, we made small talk and got to know each other. Just when I was about to ask, "Are we there yet?" she turned off the main road and stopped to unlock a gate. "Welcome to Omuzire", she said as we drove through the gate and into the bush. Darkness had fallen some time ago and my vision was limited to the things revealed by the high beams of the land cruiser. As we drove into the bush along the old farm road, it began to sink in where I was. I was in a place that I had not even imagined just six months ago, in the bushveld, in Africa.

When we pulled into camp, Johann's parents, Vellies and Clarissa, met us. Before the introductions were over, what was left of my gear was already making its way toward my tent. It took only a few seconds more before just how cold the African night can get became overtly apparent as my teeth started to chatter. You see, it was 90 degrees when I left Raleigh, North Carolina and I had packed my coat instead of wearing it. **Hint number four: always pack a small carry-on bag with what you need to be comfortable if a bag is lost.** I would have been miserable if Vellies had not been kind enough to loan me a coat. As we settled in around the fire pit, the thirty-degree weather did not seem so bad, and Vellies asked if I was ready for a delayed sundowner. I answered with an immediate affirmative and he then asked me, since I liked dark beer, if I would like to try a local dark brew. I started to ask how he knew I liked dark beer when it dawned on me that the questionnaire I had filled out months ago had determined the type of beer that was now on its way to me. That beer, and a few others along with some pleasant conversation around the fire pit, eased me in to my first evening in camp. Clarissa rang the dinner bell. It smelled wonderful when I entered the dining tent. I asked what it was and she told me it was "Bobotie", which is a spicy minced-meat pie made with kudu and gemsbok. Add a good South African wine and the result is a wonderful meal. It was one I will not forget.

The smell of fresh perked coffee drifting from the cook tent woke me early the next morning. I could have slept a few more hours, but, this being my first day in camp, I did not want to miss anything. When I stumbled into the cook tent, it was buzzing with activity. Vera was cooking and watching her three-year-old daughter Zoe. I asked where the coffee was and as she poured me a cup, she told me that she had just talked to Johann and he was only a few minutes out. While I waited for his arrival and breakfast, I had my first look at Omuzire in the daylight. The more I looked around, the better I liked it. I saw a good blend of old and new. The tents were made out of traditional canvas; the boma or fence around the fire pit was made out of reeds. All of the old was perfectly blended in with the modern solar panels that gave the camp its electricity. It was truly the best of both worlds. The warmth from my coffee cup was cutting the edge off the morning chill, and I started to wonder if my luggage would show up. I must have been deep in thought because I did not notice Johann drive up until he stopped in front of the boma. It was then I got my first glimpse of how dedicated he was to his clients. He and his tracker, Tjokkie, had left out before dawn in sub-freezing weather in an open hunting truck to get back in time for me to have a full day in camp. They looked completely frozen and miserable. I thought he stuttered for the first thirty minutes because he was shivering so badly. He thawed out during breakfast and we started getting to know each other a little bit. I realized then and there just how lucky I was. Through sheer good fortune, I had stumbled on a good booking agent and PH and, if the rest of the trip was as good as the first night and morning, I was in for the time of my life.

Cooking the old fashioned way
with a wood fired range

Fire Pit Inside the Boma

Out behind the kitchen tent

My Tent

Reed Boma

Wood Fired Water Heater

CHAPTER FOUR
Getting There

If you have ever heard the expression, "You can hardly get there from here?" they could have been talking about going to Africa. While not quite as bad as that, getting to Africa takes considerable planning and coordinating. **Hint number five: use a travel agency that specializes in African travel for hunters.** The travel agency Rick recommended to me was Gracy Travel in San Antonio, Texas. They have done nothing but first-class work on every trip I have taken to Africa. Other than a few snafus caused by the airlines themselves, I have had no problems traveling to and inside the Dark Continent. A travel agency specializing in African travel is a wealth of information. The things I found most valuable were the nuances of the local airlines, the local gun laws and needed forms, the easy to follow itinerary, and the contacts in Africa to help with problems. Let us look at each one of theses in a little more detail.

Airlines in Africa do not really operate like those in the United States. While I have had nothing but first-class service while using African based airlines, they do have their own personalities. They may only operate on certain days of the week or certain flights are only overnight with no daytime connections. The only flight to a particular airport may arrive after all the other departing flights for the day have been long gone. Some European airports are not firearm-friendly and you will want to avoid them if possible. My last trip to Africa was to Namibia and the on to Zimbabwe. There were some questions about how and if a European Union ban on firearm importation to Zimbabwe would affect hunters. My agent knew this and suggested not taking any chances by avoiding Europe. A specialist will know all of this and be able to save you time and headaches, and still get you to where you want to go.

No two countries in Africa use the same forms or permits for guns. This is one of the reasons that I suggest using a specialist in African travel for hunters. The form can be as simple as the one-page Namibian form all the way to the eight-page form used by South Africa. Some of the better agencies can help you fill forms out in advance and have your permits waiting for you. African governments are serious about their paperwork and it must be completed correctly or you will have problems. A travel agent that can help you with or handle this for you is worth their weight in gold. The transportation of guns on United States airlines is not difficult to comply with, but the regulations are somewhat fluid. A travel agency that specializes in hunters will keep you out of trouble here as well. On my first trip to Africa, I was prepared with all of my gun paperwork filled out but still apprehensive about the process. As I made my way through Namibian Customs and Immigration, I made the mistake of letting my imagination run wild with "what ifs". By the time I got to the police station inside the airport, I was nervous. The officer behind the counter was working away filling out paperwork and moving people through as fast as he could. I heard someone behind me yell up to the officer asking if he needed help. The officer looked up from his paperwork and a smile Began to form on his face as he recognized an old friend. He yelled "sure, get your backside up here". A hunter from California made his way to the front of the line and asked the officer what he needed. He told him to match people to their gun cases and have them open and ready for him. The police officer took each hunter's paperwork, checking identification, where the person was going to be hunting, how much ammunition the hunter had, and the serial numbers on the rifles. Once the information was verified, the paperwork was signed, and the hunter was allowed to go on their way. What a marvelous system.

The itinerary that I received before each of my hunts was one of the most comforting pieces of paper I had on my trip. I tend to be a nervous traveler. Not so much about the traveling itself, but I am always worrying if I am in the right place at the right time, if I am I early enough, or if I have the right paperwork, and anything else I can personally forget or screw up. This itinerary did away with all of that. It listed my travel day, telling me everything I needed to know and do. It told me how early to be at the airport, what forms to have at the ready, terminal and gate information, flight number and type of aircraft, seat assignment, where to go in the airport for customs, and on and on. If you have an overnight stay or have a long layover and want to take a day room, it had step-by-step instructions for that as well. It was my checklist and got me through my trip with minimal apprehension and effort. The itinerary even had instructions for me on non-travel days. It told me to have my PH call the airline two days before I was to leave to reconfirm my flight and seat assignment, thus helping to avoid any unexpected problems on my return trip.

My travel agent had personnel in Africa to help their clients while they were in country. When I took the whole family to Africa, our flight from the United States got to Johannesburg, South Africa after the last flight to Windhoek, Namibia and necessitated an overnight stay. I was prepared with all of the South African paperwork to claim my guns and take them to the B&B, where we were spending the night. Gravy Travel had booked our B&B and had an agent at the airport to meet us, get us through the airport, and to the B&B shuttle. Bruce's has an extensive knowledge of the airport and firearm processing procedures, and we were very confident there would be no unknown surprises. Bruce's warm disposition is definitely a plus and he has a good working relationship will all airport personnel. If a problem arises, he is well equipped to handle it and has done so if necessary. After greeting us in the baggage claim area He guided us through the airport to the police station where he arranged for my guns to be kept overnight and then to the waiting shuttle. He met us again at six in the morning took me back to the Police station and had them check my guns through to Windhoek. This man saved me hours at the airport and made what could have been a negative experience a very positive experience. Since my last trip, there has been an added feature of being met at the plane and escorted through immigrations if you want it.

Whoever you choose to help you with your travel needs to have a method for you to contact them while you are abroad. This could be an international toll-free number, or the ability to call collect. A canceled flight due to weather is not too much of an inconvenience in the U.S., where you can usually be rerouted or take a later flight. In Africa, however, a canceled flight that only goes once a week could ruin or cancel your whole trip. Your agent must be accessible for emergencies twenty-four hours per day, seven days per week, and not just during their business hours. Imagine being stranded in a foreign country in a different time zone and having to wait hours for your travel agency to open back in the United States. That is not a very comforting thought is it? Lastly, do not try to go cheap. These folks earn their money and I think I have given you some good examples of how. Feel free to check around if you like, but I think I can save you the trouble. The two times I have checked on airfare myself (I get bored rather easily), I found I could have saved a little money by doing my own booking. The best I was able to do was to trim

$150.00 off a $2500.00 fare and add eight hours to travel time and one more plane change. I decided that I was stupid for looking and have not done it since. Save yourself the headache and leave your transportation details to your PTA (professional travel agent).

Where you do have more of a choice is in the route you take. Unless you just want to take some time to visit there avoid travel through the UK or the Netherlands. Both of these are gateways to Africa, but complying with their firearm laws is more trouble than it is worth. This leaves you with two main routes, going through Frankfurt, Germany or a direct flight to Johannesburg, South Africa. They both have their advantages and disadvantages. I will try to give you enough information so that you can decide which route would work best for you. Either route takes me an average of thirty hours, including getting to the airport early and layovers.

Let's start with the direct flight to Johannesburg. If you are traveling to the southern half of Africa, chances are you will have to go through there anyway as it is a major regional hub. I live in the central part of North Carolina and have the luxury of being able to use several airports. I have flown to Johannesburg from Washington, DC and Atlanta Georgia and there is not much difference. The bad news is it is over fifteen hours in a plane from either location. Fifteen hours is a long time in a plane and it will wear you out mentally and physically. The good news is that it gets most of your traveling done in one fell swoop, and if you are one of the lucky people that can sleep on a plane, snoozing for half the flight, you are in great shape. Once you get to Johannesburg, you will probably have a short flight to your final destination. The only question left is when is your short flight? I have hit it both ways. On my first trip, I had a short layover and a few-hour flight to Windhoek that put me in camp just after dark. The last time, my flight from the United States arrived after all of the outgoing flights and I had to overnight in Johannesburg. It left from Atlanta about 8:00 pm and got to Johannesburg about 6:00 pm the next day.

That was sort of a unique experience as I had my wife and two teenage daughters with me. We knew we were going to have to overnight, but we did not know our airline would not let us have our checked bags. Me, I had my contacts lenses, change of clothes, boots, and a fresh pair of skivvies in my carry-on bag. The girls, however, decided that they would rather have books, makeup, and comfort items in their carry-on and packed their clothes. When we checked our bags upon arrival at our local airport, the check-in attendant checked our bags all the way through to our final destination. Which was fine, or so we thought. When we got to Johannesburg, the airline told us that we could not have our bags for our overnight stay because they were checked through to Windhoek, not Johannesburg. The girls were most unhappy and had to make do with what they had. I had told them my next hint but it really hadn't sunk in yet. **Hint number six: be ready for anything when you are in Africa, because, anything can happen and it usually does.** My Boy Scout motto of "Be Prepared" has served me well over the years especially in Africa.

After the girls got calmed back down, we caught our transfer to the Afton Guest House. It was only a short ride from the airport and it gave us time to look around before dinner. There was a nice trophy room and, after I grabbed a beer, I got to show off a little by identifying the animals. Even though very tired, the girls were ready to get into the bush and see animals on the hoof but not on the wall. We made our way out to the fire and tried to warm up a little in the cold South African night. The fire was not roaring as I had hoped but, rather, burned down. We soon found out why. Our evening meal was to be some prime steaks and the fire had burnt down to embers just right for cooking. The smell of the steaks grilling was about more than I could stand. I thought my stomach was going to gnaw through to my backbone before we could eat. We finally moved inside and had a nice steak dinner. I spent a little more time by the fire and then settled in for the night. We were pleasantly surprised the next morning when we got to the airport and found that our luggage was already aboard the plane. We chose a 9:45 am flight for the last leg of our journey to Windhoek. That put us at the airport around 6:00 am. This gave us time to eat and shop a little. It would also get us to Windhoek before lunch and allow us to start our long drive at a decent hour. We cleared security and headed to the food court for breakfast. I was as excited as they were. In a few short hours I would be back on the ground in Namibia, ready to start a new adventure.

Coming back, the fifteen-hour flight becomes a sixteen-hour plus flight. The only reason I can figure is that, normally, there are headwinds when you fly from east to west. There is also a little good news, even if it does require a little rationalization on your part. The flight out of Johannesburg is a late one and you are probably going to be tired from all of your adventures. If you combine these two items, you should be able to sleep for most of the trip home. If you are flying to the eastern coast of the United States, your flight will arrive early to mid-morning. Add a layover with enough time to clear immigrations and customs and another flight, you should be home by mid-day or early afternoon.

No matter how your flights work out, O.R. Tambo Airport in Johannesburg is a nice airport. It is large and has many shopping and dining opportunities. It is not hard at all to kill several hours in between flights. One of my favorite places is the upstairs sports bar. There is a great selection of malted beverages and several wide-screen televisions with sports from around the world. I find my layovers go rather quickly while I am there. The only compliant—and it is a minor one—is the airport always seems to be under construction. Air traffic in Africa seems to be growing at a steady rate and the airport keeps getting bigger. The only reason I mention it is that for the next leg of your journey you will probably be on a smaller plane. With the larger jets taking all of the gates, you will probably have to board a shuttle bus and take a short ride out to the tarmac to board your flight. The specialized travel agent you use should tell you this, but you should be at the gate early. Boarding the shuttle can be unorganized and time consuming. **Hint number seven: plan your carry on for small planes.** Almost everyone coming to Africa on the large planes has carry-on baggage that fits the large planes easily but not so well on the small planes. Even if someone can get their large piece in the overhead bin, it will leave very little room for yours. Being prepared for this can help if you are not one of the first ones on the shuttle and then the plane. Plan ahead for this and save yourself some trouble later. It could keep the valuables that you did not want checked sitting on the tarmac in an unlocked bag waiting to be checked planeside.

The next route, and my favorite I might add, is the route through Frankfurt Germany. This route might take a little longer but it breaks up the time in the air and helps you be acclimated to the local time zone. This might sound too good to be true but if you can sleep in a plane even a little bit it works. I took this route on my second trip to Africa and was somewhat skeptical, but, I promise you, I will go this way, if at all possible, on all future trips. This is how it works.

My trip was going to start by going from Raleigh NC to Atlanta, GA, then from Atlanta to Frankfurt, and finally to Windhoek. My problems started in Raleigh after I got to the airport and found out that storms had delayed all flights in and out of Raleigh. I tried reading to take my mind of things and when that didn't work I tried daydreaming about my upcoming leopard hunt. I wondered if I was up to the task of my first dangerous game hunt or if Mr. Spots would even show up. I could not wait to be there. Darn it, I interrupted my own daydream. Now I was back to thinking about thunderstorms. Getting there was turning out to be a problem. How could I get there if the storms would not go away? I know I'll call my wife at work and get her to look at the local radar on her computer. Not good. The line of storms is slow-moving and will be here a while. I watch the rain pour for a while and decide I'll get wife to take another look. Not good. She threatened me with bodily harm if I do not leave her alone and let her finish her work. I walked back down to the bar to have a beer. That helped and, while I was sitting there, I came up with my next hint. It is probably one of my better suggestions. **Hint number eight: never bother your wife with your travel problems if you are going on the trip without her.** Your complaints may cause you a bigger problem than the one you currently have. I filed this revelation away for future reference and headed back to the gate.

The rain finally cleared and I caught my flight to Atlanta, but my one-hour-and-fifty-minute layover turned into a thirty-minute layover. I scrambled to get through one of America's busiest airports in order to catch my connecting flight. I just had time to grab a couple of snacks and bottles of water before I got to the gate. I almost did not have enough time to comply with my **hint number nine: on each leg of your flight, check to make sure your baggage was transferred.** It sounds like overkill, but, if something has happened with your baggage and the airline finds out about it early, the better chance they have at correcting the problem without inconveniencing you. My baggage had been transferred, and I considered that the start of a change in my luck. That proved to be true as my flight to Germany was pleasant and, best of all, uneventful.

I arrived in Frankfurt at 9:20 am local time. Having slept a little on the plane, my body really did not have to make a shift to the local time zone. It was just like sleeping after a late night out. Since my Air Namibia flight did not leave to 10:45 pm, I had my travel agent arrange a day room for me at one of the local hotels. What is a day room, you ask? I had never heard of one either, until both Rick and then Gracy Travel suggested one, and it is my **hint number ten: if your flight schedule allows it, get a day room**.

A day room is a room you rent for just the daytime hours and not overnight. It was going to be nice to get out of the airport for eight to ten hours and take a shower, relax and get some non-airline food. It is very simple to do. Your baggage is not a problem, since it stays checked, and therefore locked up at the airport. All you have to do is go through customs and immigration, hop into the shuttle, check in, and relax. It took me longer to find the customs and immigration than it did to go through it. The officer asked what I was doing and I told him I was taking a day room before catching a late flight. He looked at my ticket and passport, and I was done. Another option is to put your carry-on bag in an airport locker and use the time to sightsee around Frankfurt. Either way, you get out of the airport and can stretch your legs. If neither of those suits you, it is possible to spend the whole day looking around the Frankfurt airport. It is that big. If you do take a day room, be sure and double check the shuttle schedule when you register at the hotel. You do not want to miss the last shuttle of the day and have to find a taxi. Since I had opted to take a day room, I proceeded to enjoy myself. I had a nice long shower and then a short nap. The restaurant was nice and not too expensive and I was able to try some of the local food. I took a short walk, and then I headed back to the room, to relax in front of the TV. One other advantage of a day room that I really enjoy is the full-sized bathroom that you have all to yourself, a most welcome break form the tiny lavatory on the plane.

My trusty itinerary said to be back three hours before my departure, so I took the 6:30 shuttle back to the airport. Even though I located the Air Namibia desk before I left that morning, I figured a little extra time would not hurt. When I walked past the Air Namibia desk, I noticed a group of people talking in front of it. I did not think much of it and went for a cup of coffee and window-shopping. I was gone about an hour and, when I got back, there was between one hundred fifty and two hundred people in line. Not wanting to appear as if I did not know what I was doing, I got in line with them. I do not know if I did the right thing or not, but I got on the plane with no problems and we left at 10:45 on the dot. I think I dozed off in the middle of a movie somewhere around midnight. The flight attendants woke us up about 6:00 for breakfast and to hand out declaration forms for customs. **Hint number eleven: fill out the declaration forms before you leave the plane; it will save you time and effort.** The forms were simple and straightforward it took no time to fill them out and I was done well before we landed. If you have questions, ask the flight attendants. They can help you fill out the forms if you need them to. We touched down about 7:45 am and, once again, I was able to keep my normal sleep pattern and had no jet lag whatsoever.

Windhoek Hosea Kutako International Airport is small but modern airport. You will disembark on the tarmac and have a short walk to immigrations and customs. I was a little concerned when I got inside and saw the long line at the non-Namibian citizen line. There were two officers in the non-citizen line, about four others in the Namibian citizen line, and two more in the African Union line. I figured, ok, so they are taking good care of their citizens, good for them, and I settled in for a wait. Much to my amazement, as soon as the other lines cleared one of the officers came out from behind the desk and diverted sections of our long line to each of the other stations. Talk about service with a smile. I was very impressed with the professionalism, efficiency, and courteousness shown by these immigration officers. I handed them my passport and forms from the plane, they looked them over, checked my face with my passport (managing not to laugh at my picture), and sent me on my way. If you checked "nothing to declare" on your customs form, you were done as soon as you picked up your luggage. As I mentioned earlier, the firearms registration process is simple and painless. The time I stepped off the plane to the time I was ready to leave was less than an hour. One other thing to note here is if you do not understand something just ask. Whether you ask the flight attendants or the officials inside, all were willing to help and things go much quicker with correctly-filled-out forms.

The trip in reverse is almost as nice. There is an overnight flight from Windhoek to Frankfurt, so you can sleep your regular nighttime schedule. The biggest change is the layover for the flight back to the United States is just a few hours. It is enough time to navigate the airport and stretch your legs and it gets you back to the United States at a decent hour. Allowing for the time change, and if you live on the east coast, you could be home in time for dinner that same day.

Once you get in country, there is a possibility you may have to take a private charter to get to camp. This is one of those good news/bad news situations. The good news is you get to camp quickly and get to start your hunt that much sooner. The bad news is the cost is ridiculously expensive. On my last trip, I went to Zimbabwe for a Cape buffalo hunt and I had to make a choice of how to get to camp. The choices were an eight to nine hour drive if I could find someone going that way or take a charter flight. As much as I hate spending money if I do not have to, I chose to fly, mostly because no one from camp was passing anywhere near the airport that I flew into, and partially because eight hours in a safari truck over rough roads was not a pleasant thought. In reality, if I drove to camp, it would be between 9:00 pm and 10:00 pm before I got to camp, and it would require wasting a whole day traveling.

You have two options of chartering your flight into camp, through your specialty travel agent or through your Safari operator or PH. I recommend using your Safari operator because of the opportunity to share flights. **Hint number twelve: if possible, share a charter flight with another hunter**. This will cut down on your cost considerably. The rate for the plane was the same if it was one or two people in it. I made the mistake of not choosing the airport for my commercial flight based on the probability of being able to share the charter flight with another hunter. This is **hint number thirteen: check with your Safari operator to find out if they have any other clients flying in and to which airport they are flying.** If you can match your destination to theirs, the better your odds of being able to share a plane and cutting your cost by at least half. A Safari operator should be more than happy to help you arrange to share a flight. If they succeed, the result is a happy client. If they do not succeed but give it a good effort, they still have a happy client. They can't lose no matter what the outcome is. One more reason to use your Safari operator is they will use a charter service that they trust to take good care of their client. If the hunter gets to camp in a bad mood because of bad service from a charter company that the Safari operator recommended, it could be a bad week for all involved.

I'll bet that that the thought of an extra day in camp never crossed your mind as a way to save money, but it is possible. If a charter flight is coming to camp one day after your scheduled departure, consider staying an extra day. Do the math and see what works best. It could be less expensive to spend an extra day than to pay for the whole charter. Just remember to do this before you book your commercial airfare. One last nicety about a charter service – there will probably be someone on staff to help you through the airport. When I arrived in Zimbabwe, an employee of the charter service met me at the immigrations and customs line. He checked to make sure I had the correct paperwork and escorted me through the whole process. Once we cleared immigration, he helped me claim my baggage and get all of the police paperwork processed. After the police station, we rolled right past everyone else and into the private aviation section of the airport, where I had a short wait for my flight. The airport in Victoria Falls Zimbabwe is not a large place, but it sure was nice to have a private guide to get me through it.

The best thing about the charted flight is that it is in a small plane. When I left the airport in Vic Falls, the pilot asked if I had ever seen the falls, to which I replied that I had not. With that, he turned and headed for the falls. I probably do not need to tell you that the view of

Added bonus of a charter flight, lookind down into Victoria Falls

Aerial view of Vic falls

Victoria Falls from the air is phenomenal sight. He banked the plane for me to get a better view and I could see down in the canyons carved out by the water rushing over the edge of the falls. I am sure that the view from the ground is awesome, but being able to see the whole thing at the same time is very cool as well. The thing that you cannot see from the ground is the way the water had cut its path through the canyon in a zigzag pattern until it finally works its way onto level ground. Flying at an altitude where the animals are still visible was a new experience for me. While I saw only small groups, it was easy to imagine the large herds of plains animals of times gone by. It was also all too easy to see the huge plumes of smoke in all directions. Some of the fires were accidental or caused by something in nature, but others were set on purpose. Poachers often set fires to herd animals into a specific area. If the animals are concentrated in a particular area, it makes finding them that much easier for the poachers. It also ties up the rangers by putting them on fire duty instead of anti-poaching duty. I know that fire is nature's way of rejuvenating the landscape, but to see fire set to the detriment of nature was truly disappointing. Between trying to read the book I had with me and staring out the window, the flight passed quickly. With approximately 20 minutes remaining of our flight, the pilot directed my attention to what looked to me like

a large plateau and told me that is where camp is. As we approached, we gave the camp a quick buzz to let them know we were there and headed toward the landing strip. When we popped back up over the trees, I could see a wide level strip of grass in the middle of trees and bush. I could

My chartered plane and the grass landing strip cut out of the bush

only imagine how much manpower it took to clear that big a piece of land out of the dense bush that surrounded the airstrip.

Bush pilots themselves are sort of an enigma. Most are more than capable of being a commercial pilot, but they choose to fly tiny planes to faraway places for just for the love of flying. I have often wondered how bush pilots could find such a small spot in the vastness of the African wilderness in the old days before GPS and other modern navigation aids. Were they able to identify unmistakable landmarks or did they just have an internal compass that always got them to where they needed to go? There is one other thing that I have never been able to figure out about bush pilots. How is it that a bush pilot can put a plane down smooth as silk on a lake or grass landing strip, but a commercial pilot has to bounce a plane a few times before it settles to the ground? If anyone knows, I would appreciate an answer sometime. This pilot was no exception; he sat the plane down smoothly and taxied us over to one corner of the landing strip. It only took us a few minutes to unload and secure the plane.

Due to my commercial flight schedule, we had arrived at camp too late for the pilot to return before dark and he was going to have to spend the night. Even though it should not have, it surprised me that the commercial airport that I had flown into earlier had no night-landing capabilities. I guess I should have remembered a variation of **hint number six**, which I'll call **hint number six-a: be ready for anything – Africa is full of surprises, and will spring them on you at any time**. Although be ready for anything might be a little overkill, be adaptable may be a better phrase and is advisable. Anyway, the pilot and I found a shady spot and waited for the people from camp to show up with our ride back to camp.

Now that you have thought about how you are going to get to Africa, we need to make a few more stops before we leave the country. If you do not already have one, you are going to need a passport, and if you do not have them, you are going to need vaccinations. Let's start with the passport since it is the less painful of the two. You need to get a passport photo taken. This service is available at most AAA club locations, at your local photographer, or some larger camera shops. The photograph should be two inches by two inches and be in color. Next, call your local post office to find out if they do passports, since not all post offices offer passports. You should also ask what forms of payment is needed as that may vary as well. After you get your picture taken and it is the right size, take it to the appropriate post office. Fill out the paperwork and have everything sent away for processing. It will take several months, unless you want to pay for an expeditor. I recommend starting at least nine months out just to allow for any hang-ups' that might occur. If you already have a passport make sure that, you have at least three or four blank pages in it. Certain countries will not allow you in if you have fewer than three blank pages.

Next stop is the United States Center for Disease Control website. Go to the travel section and plug in the name of the country to which you will be traveling. From here you can find out which vaccinations you need and what kind if any malaria prophylaxis the CDC recommends. If you need vaccinations, I recommend scheduling an appointment six to nine months out. This will give your physician time to get any vaccines he does not have in stock. It will also give you time to address any negative reaction to the vaccine that you might have. While you are at the doctor's office, discuss the anti-malaria medications that are ok for your area of travel. There are several medicines listed for each area and most of them have side effects. The side effects range from sun sensitivity, to having vivid nightmares, to the frequency and duration of the treatment, to cost. Alright, the last two are not side effects but they might make a difference in your decision. While you have your doctor's attention, tell him you would like a course of a broad-spectrum antibiotic. This will come in handy if you encounter the type of stomach distress that you can contract by drinking from the local water supply. Have your physician make a note on your file that you will be calling thirty days out to ask for your two prescriptions. That way, when he forgets that you had the conversation, you can tell him where his notes are

CHAPTER FIVE

What to Take

Ask a dozen people what to take to Africa and you'll get a dozen different answers. Combine the dozen different answers and you'll get **hint number fourteen: combine all of the "what to take" list you get, remove any duplicate items, and then adjust for personal preference.** This will give you a list that is specific to African travel and one that covers a broad spectrum of items, one that you can personalize to your individual taste and needs. At the very least, combine the list, I give you (which is my combination of list I received) with the list of your booking agent and your PH. If there is something on a list that you do not understand the importance of, ask a question and find out. I guarantee it was important to someone. While you are preparing your list, keep in mind the airline-imposed weight restrictions on your baggage, and that one of your two allowed bags is your gun case. In the one bag with your clothing, you also have to carry your up to eleven pounds of ammunition. This leaves thirty-nine pounds for everything else.

Let's start with your carry-on bag. Be practical and think through the items that you choose to pack. What are more comfortable than your casual clothes that you wear around hunting camp? Pick something with which you can do double duty, meaning clothing that you could hunt or just relax in. Count this as one of your three or four changes of clothes (long pants and long-sleeved shirt) and put them into your carry-on along with your hunting boots, two pairs of hiking socks, a change of underwear, and a jacket. Next, pack your toiletries in small, travel-size quantities and a percentage of any medications that you may need. That should leave you room for your optics and camera equipment. If you pack in this fashion, you should be able to complete your hunt even if other luggage goes missing.

If your luggage does go missing and you must have some replacement items inform whoever is picking you up at the airport that you would like to stop at a pharmacy or store of some kind on the way to camp. Go ahead and pick up the essentials before you leave whatever city is closest to the airport. It would be better to have some duplication if your baggage shows up later than to have to leave camp and drive hours back to town if it does not. If during the flight you suddenly remember something you forgot, get it before leaving town as well. On one flight, fleas or some biting insect on the plane besieged me. I had no hydrocortisone or anti-itch cream with me; I asked Johann if we could stop on the way out of town. With a three-minute stop, I had a supply of hydrocortisone to last me for the rest of the trip. Without that quick stop, I would have been miserable for days and probably would have wasted a day of hunting going back to town for the medicine.

For the rest of your list, I would suggest the following items of clothing: three additional long-sleeved shirts, plus one t-shirt, two long pants and one pair of shorts, polar fleece vest and/or sweater, one additional pair of wool socks and two pairs of cotton socks, two pairs of underwear, one hat or cap, one knit cap, and one pair of light leather gloves. Lastly, take a long-sleeved silk thermal top for a base layer or sleeping in, and take an extra pair of boots. Let me explain the reason behind my list. First, in the arid climate of southern Africa, it gets cold at night. I have seen the water frozen in the birdbaths outside my tent on more than one occasion. Your long pants and long-sleeved shirts will be very welcome on the cold rides in an open safari truck. Your jacket should be windproof, if possible, and sized to fit over your shirt, vest, and sweater if necessary. The ability to add and remove layers will be very important as the temperature varies throughout the day. The dry air in Africa allows for tremendous temperature swings. I have seen forty to fifty degree changes between the high and low temperatures of the day. These large temperature changes are the reason for one pair of short pants and a short sleeve or t-shirt.

During your mid-day break you will want these while you relax around camp. You may want to consider wearing a pair of tennis shoes or sneakers while you are on the plane. Changing from your boots and wool socks to dry cotton socks and a pair of sneakers felt awfully good to my feet during my lunch breaks and allowed my boots to dry out a little. A wide-brimmed hat or a ball cap that can keep the sun out of your eyes while shooting can be very helpful. A brimmed hat has the added advantage of keeping the sun off the rest of your face and neck but sometimes can be troublesome getting through thick brush. The choice is up to you and you may want to take both, since neither weighs very much. As far as the quantity of clothing goes, remember that you should have access to a daily laundry service. The items I left in the laundry hamper in the morning were washed, dried, ironed, and left folded on my bed that evening when I returned from hunting.

Here are a few more things to consider in picking out your African wardrobe. The bushveld is very tough on clothing and full of thorns, briars, and lots of other sharp things. While modern fleece-type materials are soft, warm, lightweight, and comfortable, they are also prone to letting thorns pass through to your skin unimpeded and picking up burrs and nettles. I recommend them only for under layers. Your outer layer should be of a good-quality, tightly woven material that will help turn the many thorns you will encounter. What works best for me are pants and shirts made from a cotton canvas or cotton duck, not the heavy-weight material used to make tarps, but a lighter weight typically used in good-quality hunting or work clothing. This material will protect you from many of the ouchies that you will encounter in the African bush. Another option is upland hunting clothing. If you have some of the warm season, lighter-weight clothing that is quiet, it will work as well.

Your personal taste and where you are hunting will dictate whether you wear traditional safari colors of tan and green or modern camouflage. At the time of this writing, some countries such as Zimbabwe do not allow modern hunting camouflage, and none of them that I know of allows the military type. The safest and best thing to do is ask your PH. His recommendation is important because he knows the area where you will be hunting. He can tell you what shades of green and tan work best, or if a particular camouflage pattern is more effective than another is. His advice could also save you some money by keeping you from going out and buying the wrong things or duplicating something that you might already have.

Toiletry items are highly personalized and unique to each of us individually, so I will not attempt to tell you want you need, but, rather, make some general suggestions. For simplicity's sake, and to save space and weight, I recommend an unscented shampoo and body wash combination. Unscented antiperspirant is also a very good idea. There are several good ones on the market, and not smelling like a flower pot or spring rain will help you stalk closer to game giving you an easier shot. For shaving in camp, I recommend using your unscented body wash to make lather for shaving. For aftershave lotion, use an unscented hand lotion; it will also come in handy if your skin chaps in the dry air.

Unless you are one of those rare individuals that always tans and never burns, sunscreen is an absolute necessity. Finding one that is unscented has been a problem though. If there has been no added scent, the odor of the various chemicals is still there. Another problem I have with sunscreen is I personally cannot stand for it to leave an oily or sticky residue on my skin. These problems resolved themselves when I tried a sunscreen with an alcohol base. The alcohol evaporates quickly, leaving very little residue and, in a short time, no odor. A good rule is to apply your sunscreen twice daily, once when you wake up and again during your lunch break. You will be miserable hunting under the African sun if you already have a case of sunburn; I can tell you this from first-hand experience.

Now for **hint number fifteen: since most of the above items come in larger quantities, buy some small empty bottles so that you can transfer some from the larger bottles into them for your carry-on bag**. Just make sure the bottles are below the three-ounce size as required by current airport security regulations. This last item is just a suggestion, but one that I take with me, and that is saline nasal spray. The air is very dry and the saline keeps my sinuses moist, and it helps me fend off headaches and sleep more comfortably. The saline spray was also helpful when it came time to wash the fine African dust out of my sinuses at the end of the day.

Traveling with your medications is easy if you follow a few simple suggestions. First, though, is **hint number sixteen: save one old prescription bottle for each medication you take.** When people travel with any kind of medication, I always recommend keeping them in the original container. The original bottle could save you a lot of explaining to a customs agent who is unsure of what a group of unlabeled pills is doing in your luggage. Having the extra bottle allows you to split your medications into two groups, one for your carry-on bag and one for your checked luggage, and still have them in the original container. The label of the extra bottle will also facilitate the accurate filling of a prescription should one become lost. If you do not want to carry extra bottles, get your doctor to write you an extra prescription for everything and take them with you. The same advice goes for any over-the-counter medications you are taking. Put them in two different bags and leave them in the original packaging. I would also recommend taking one extra week's worth of medicine just in case. (If you ask, "in case of what?", see **hint number six** and **six-a**.)

If there is one other category on which I would want you to double up, that would be eyewear. If you have them, take two pairs of prescription eyewear, and the same goes for contact lenses and sunglasses. If you do not have an old pair of glasses that you can use, consider buying an extra pair. You can do this fairly inexpensively if you start looking early. There are websites and major eyewear retailers that run specials on a somewhat regular basis. If you wear soft contacts, you are in good shape. Just take an extra pair or two, and if you have to use them, just order replacements when you get back. I must be one of the last few people on earth that refuse to switch to soft contact lenses. I love my old-fashioned hard contacts but to have an extra pair is quite expensive. So, what did I do? I scheduled my regular optometrist appointment five months out from my trip. It turned out that my prescription had changed very little and I kept my old lenses as back up. Another option for hard lens wearers would be to get a free trial pair of soft lenses from your optometrist. If you can stand the aggravation of wearing them, it could save your trip.

On my first trip to Namibia, I was rinsing my lenses off during lunch. I put the first one in, blinked a few times, and moved on to the second lens. When I got the second lens in and my blinked away the wetting solution, I noticed things looked fuzzy. A quick close of each eye revealed that my first contact was now missing. I must have blinked or wiped it out of my eye when I was removing the excess wetting solution. I quickly proceeded to panic and dropped to my knees to look for my missing lens. After crawling around on the floor of my tent, looking in my shirt pockets, on the towel I wiped my face with, and just about every other place I could think of, I deemed it lost forever. I would have to wear my glasses for the rest of the hunt. That would be a problem because I did not have any sunglasses to fit over my regular glasses. I resigned myself to just having to tough it out. As I sat through lunch, feeling sorry for myself, I suddenly remembered that I had stuck my old lens in my toiletry kit for just such an emergency. The old contact got me through the rest of the trip just fine. That one little piece of plastic saved my safari. You might think an extra pair of sunglasses is a little much, but I can assure it is not. Africa has a way of making things disappear, getting scratches on them, or just plain breaking them. The decision is up to you, but I think it is a cheap, lightweight insurance policy.

The next item is another cheap lightweight insurance item. It is a small pocket-sized first aid kit. You do not need anything major, as your PH will have a heavy-duty first aid kit on the truck. It is more important that you keep this in your pocket. You need a few Band-Aids, some antibiotic ointment, and blister covers. I particularly like the Band-Aid brand blister packs as they go on and stay on. Even if your boots are well-broken-in, you can get blisters. When I was in Zimbabwe, we were in very sandy terrain for a good portion of each day. The boots I was wearing were two years old and very broken-in and I still got some blisters started on both feet. The blister pads went on over the area that was starting to blister. It cushioned it, allowed no more friction, and this kept the makings of the blister from becoming a full-blown problem. Since I had the kit in my pocket, I could take a short break, sit down, and fix the problem before it really started. The bandages and antibiotic kept cuts, splinters and the like clean and protected until I could get back to camp and fix them on a more permanent basis. I know that I am not the only accident-prone hunter out there and especially in Africa, an ounce of prevention really is worth two pounds of cure.

Now that I have talked about cheap, lightweight insurance items, let's talk about some that are maybe not so cheap. Well in advance of your departure date, call your health insurance provider and tell them where you are going. Find out if it is possible and what you have to do to have international coverage. Most companies have provisions for their insured to get coverage overseas, but it is up to you to know how to do it. Be sure to take good notes while you talk to your insurance provider, or, better yet, get them to send you an instruction sheet on what to do while you are abroad. If there is no instruction sheet available, have them send you just the section of your policy that explains what to do overseas.

Another area that I want to discuss is medical evacuation insurance. This insurance will get you back to a hospital in the United States if you are injured. The jets will come complete with a medical staff and equipment to get you back to your hospital of choice. Some of the services are even able to pick you up in the bush if you have an accident in hunting camp. Medjet Assist and Global Rescue are two of the many companies that provide this type of insurance. Check with your insurance company to see if they recommend or have a working relationship with a particular company. If they do not, do your own research and pick the one that best suits your needs. I am not endorsing one company or the other. I simply want to make you aware of their existence. Whether or not you need the insurance is up to you. My rule of thumb is if I am traveling with family, it is absolutely necessary. If I am by myself, I am a little more wishy-washy. If I am hunting plains game, I might not buy the insurance. If I were hunting dangerous game, I would be more inclined to do so.

The last form of insurance I want to bring up is trip insurance. There are two types of trip insurance. Regular trip insurance covers you if, for some reason, you are not able to take your trip. Trip-interruption insurance covers any expenses you incur if you become stranded or delayed. If you are foot loose and fancy free, I would not worry about the first one and might consider the second. If you have elderly or ailing family members or a narrow window of time in which to take your trip, I would probably think about buying both. If you buy a policy, be sure it says, in clear concise terms, what you think it does. Do not think that because it seems logical that something is covered, that it actually is covered. If you have a specific worry about being able to take a trip, mention it in specific terms to the policy salesperson. If you spell it out, you should have no unexpected consequences.

I know that I am going to open up myself to a lot of criticism and aggravation in this next section, but I am going to talk about cameras anyway. Since today's technology is changing faster and faster. Today's computer-aided cameras will probably be outdated before you read this. So, I am just going to speak in generalities based on my experience with photography and Africa. First, because of your weight restrictions, smaller is better. I have the old 35-mm SLR cameras and equipment that I dearly love and I even took it with me on one trip to Africa. I did not use it even once; it is just too heavy to carry around. I also took a pocket-sized digital camera.

I bought the camera especially for the trip, and here is what I looked for. First, I wanted a high-resolution camera, one that took pictures that I could enlarge if I wanted to when I got home. Secondly, I wanted a high optical zoom with a digital multiplier on top of the optical zoom. An optical zoom uses the camera lens to magnify objects; a digital zoom uses the cameras computer chip to enlarge the objects it sees. The camera I chose had a 10X optical zoom and then a 3X on top of the optical zoom. Translated, that means I could magnify an object ten times with the lens of the camera. If I needed more, I could use the computer chip to triple that. I also wanted a large-view screen on the back of the camera. This was a blessing to my aging eyesight. The only thing that my camera does not have that I really, really wish it did was through the lens viewing. In bright sunlight, glare makes it is difficult for me to quickly acquire the subject of my photo using the viewing screen on the back of the camera. As a direct result of that, I missed the opportunity to get pictures of several animals that were only visible for short glimpses or that were well camouflaged. I just could not see them well enough to get the picture.

Here are a few other things that you might want to consider. How long will it take your digital camera to start up? If it is too long, you just might miss the fleeting opportunity at a great picture. Shutter response time can be another problem. Some cameras have a lag between the time the shutter release is pushed and when the picture is actually snapped. If you are taking nothing but posed or set-up pictures, this is not normally a problem. It is a problem if you are trying to take a picture of an elephant crossing narrow road just in front of you.

The ability to take video is another plus for a digital camera; that is, if you are quick minded enough to use it. After I took my buffalo in Zimbabwe, we were going for an afternoon of sand grouse shooting. My PH, Phillip Smythe, stopped the truck about fifty yards away from a group of vultures surrounding a buffalo that a group of lions had killed early during the day. I broke out my camera to take a few pictures. I had just begun taking them when one of the lions busted out of the nearby brush. It seemed that he had taken offence at the buzzards taking a few bites out of his leftovers and was chasing them away. I started taking pictures as fast as I could push the button. It was not until the lion was returning to resume his

This lion did not like the vultures snacking on his bufalo

nap in the nearby shade that I remembered that I could have been taking video of the whole encounter. Boy, did I feel stupid. I can only hope that I remember the video feature in time to use it on any future encounters.

Another advantage in using digital cameras is the ability to store a lot of pictures on a small memory card. This can be a blessing, but it can also be a curse. We found out a little-known fact about digital memory cards the hard way on our family trip to Africa. Memory cards can and sometimes do fail. My oldest daughter was using a four gigabyte during the trip. When we got home and she tried to download her pictures, we got an error message and then memory-corrupted messages. We tried buying software, taking the card to a digital photo processor, and even tried a few witch doctors and shamans, but she ended up losing a lot of her pictures. We were just lucky that her sister had shot pictures in most of the same locations and the content was pretty much the same. In the end, Kris had pictures that went with her memories. They were just not her pictures but were pictures taken by her sister. The moral of this story is to use more cards of smaller memory capacity. This will reduce your exposure (if you'll pardon the play on words) to losing pictures. On future trips, I am going to take two memory cards to use for my trophy photos. I will take a set of pictures with one card and then repeat the process with the other card in the camera. This might seem like a little overkill but I want pictures to go with my memories.

There is one other option if you like techno gadgets. There are stand-alone storage devices that you can download your pictures to at the end of every day. If you were to download your pictures and do not delete them from your memory card, this would also be a reasonable back-up system. These gadgets also give you the ability to look at your pictures at the end of the day without using up your camera batteries. I think this is important enough to make it my **hint number 17: use more small-capacity memory cards, instead of fewer large-capacity memory cards, or back up your photographs.** It might save you a lot of grief.

Most people will take reading material on a long trip, and a trip to Africa should be no exception. I want to suggest a slight twist on taking reading material. While you are deciding what reading material to take, think about buying one or two books in hardback. If you are a magazine reader, pick up a few top-shelf magazines like "Gray's" or "Sporting Classics". Why, you might ask? I'll tell you why. Most camps have very little reading material in their library and any addition would be greatly appreciated. Put your name, address, e-mail, or phone number in them and the date of your trip. You might just make some new friends that way. If someone in camp is without something to read and finds your contribution to the library enjoyable, they just might contact you when they get back, and you have a new friend. Contributing to the camp library is also a nice way of saying thank you to your host. You might think that a book or magazine would not have much effect or even be noticed by a large safari company and you might be right. I will, however, guarantee that an owner operator will notice it. In the smaller operations, little things are very much noticed. How people remember you is up to you. Me, I prefer to be remembered fondly. If the picking up of a book or magazine a year or so down the road can make that happen, I'm all for it.

The last little thing I want to cover in the duplicate, cheap, and insurance department is paperwork. **Hint number eighteen: make two copies of all paperwork, and keep them in separate places.** What I mean by paperwork is your passport, credit cards, itinerary (three copies), driver's license, customs form 4457, medical insurance information, firearms forms, contact information, and anything else that you would cause trouble if you can't find it. Do not forget to copy both sides of everything. Your credit card emergency phone numbers are on the back, and, if you lose the card, you're going to want that number to cancel and replace the card. If any company has toll-free numbers or phone numbers other than those listed on the card, be sure to write those down as well. You want to be able to cover all of your bases should the need arise. Leave the third copy of your itinerary with someone at home, just in case he or she has to find you. If there is an emergency and you have to be contacted, it is a lot easier to find you if there is a paper trail saying where you have been and where you are going to be. When you arrive in camp, take one set of your copies, remove the credit card information and give it to your PH or camp manager. If there is an accident and you are disabled or unconscious, all of your relevant information is on file in camp.

The last category in the "what to take" chapter is just a hodge-podge of oddball items that I think might require a little explanation. The first is bedroom slippers. I take bedroom slippers for two reasons. The first is my feet get tired on the long flight over and back. I stick the slippers in my carry-on and, easy as pie, my feet are comfortable in no time. The second is the floor of the tent or chalet if it is cold at night. If my feet get cold on a midnight bathroom break, it takes me that much longer to get back to sleep. A money belt is something else that I would get for my trip. It worries me if I have to carry around large amounts of money for any reason, but not because I am afraid of theft; it is far more likely that I would lose it somewhere. Last time I checked, it is fairly difficult to lose something if it is secured around your body and inside your clothes.

The next subject is food. If you have a favorite snack or treat that you like, and you can buy it commercially prepared, bring it if you want. Do not bring homemade food. It will likely be confiscated and disposed of. One of my favorites is trail mix. I bring some to take with me in the truck. It is quick-and-easy energy after a long stalk. One other thing that I like to bring are flavor packets for bottled water. One of these in a bottle of cold water on the way home or with a field lunch is a welcome change of pace.

A lens pen and a laser bore sight are two more things that you might want to think about taking. Even with lens covers on your scope, the fine dust in the African bushveld will find a way to coat your optics. A few flicks of a lens pen and you are good to go. Since the amount of ammunition you can take with you is limited, a laser bore sight can save a lot of it. Even the best scopes sometimes lose their zero while you are traveling. If you have the bore sight, you can re-zero your rifle with just one shot. What, you do not know how to re-zero with just one shot? Let me enlighten you. This is **hint number nineteen. Using the bore sight get as close to zero as possible and leave the scope's adjustment caps off. Use enough sandbags to get the rifle very stable and then fire one shot. The shot should be on the paper since you used a bore sight. Now make sure you can see the bullet hole using your scope. Return the rifle to the original point of aim, the bull's-eye, and anchor the rifle into the sandbag as securely as possible. Have your PH turn the dials on your scope so that the crosshairs go to where the bullet hole is. Now your rifle is back to zero.** It really makes sense, once you think about it. Instead of moving the point of impact to where the crosshairs are looking, often by guessing how many clicks, you are moving the crosshairs to the point of impact without the guesswork.

The new type of hearing devices that amplify low sounds and dampen loud noises are the best thing since sliced bread. If you are my age and were introduced to the shooting sports before hearing protection was common, it is hard to hear your PH whisper instructions to you. The amplification feature is a fantastic aid and I am not constantly repeating the phrase, "What did you say?" While the dampening features are adequate, they are not the best available. I, for one, am more than happy to make the trade off to gain the advantage in hearing. The type of shell carrier you pick is more important than you think. While the choice is up to you, I like a five-round leather holder on my belt and a five-round pocket pack in my pants pocket. Whatever type you chose, be sure that they will not allow the rounds to bang together. It is extremely difficult to stalk an animal if you clink or clank with every step. Just a note – do not worry about having to flip back to this chapter to find items; I have put them in the master list at the end of the book.

CHAPTER SIX

Hunting Tools

Before I really get started in the chapter, I want to make it clear that this chapter is about guns that use cartridges, not black powder, or archery equipment. While I hunt with both of those items, I do it so infrequently that I should never give anyone advice on either black powder or archery hunting. Both are capable and both have been used and used successfully in Africa. If either is what you like to hunt with, by all means, take and use them. The only advice I will offer is in the selection of a PH or Safari operator. When considering either, and before you select a date or send a deposit, tell them what you want to hunt with and especially how you like to hunt. Then, get multiple references for the type of hunt you just described. If they only have one reference that tells you that they have not done much of this type of hunting. If the reference is a glowing one, and you are willing to risk it, give them a chance. Every PH I have met has been willing to do whatever it takes to make their client happy and wants you to succeed. There is one other thing that you and regular gun hunters need to work out in advance with your PH. That is whether you want your PH to take an anchoring shot on your animal if the hit looks to be poor. With the limited energy available to black powder and archery hunters (smaller caliber rifle hunters as well), shot placement is more than critical. Remember that if you hit the animal and do not recover it, you still pay for it. So, discuss anchoring shots thoroughly. That said, let's move on to what I do know a little about.

The first question on every one's mind, when you talk about hunting in Africa, is what caliber ought to be used. The answer is easy: it is the largest caliber you can shoot WELL. Notice the emphasis on WELL. The trigger on a .600 Nitro express only takes a few pounds of pressure and no practice to pull. Getting the bullet to go where you want it and to do that consistently is a completely different matter. That said, a .270 Winchester in skilled hands will do just fine on plains game and is, in fact the minimum recommended caliber in most places. Most hunters who hunt whitetail deer already own a perfectly capable African rifle. Whether it is the previously mentioned .270 or the .30-06, .308, or larger, it will kill plains game just fine. You just have to put the bullet where it counts.

If you are hunting dangerous game, that is a whole different story. The legal minimum in most countries is the venerable .375 Holland and Holland, with a special exception for my personal favorite, the 9.3x62 Mauser. What I want you to take away from this chapter is not what caliber I think you or anyone else should shoot, but that you can put whatever caliber bullet you choose where it needs to go in a consistent manner. In addition to putting the bullet where it needs to go time after time, there are a handful of things I think are important and you should know about. If Africa is an excuse for a new rifle (I am currently holding at three and hoping for more), I'll give you a few helpful hints along the way based on what I have learned, not just my personal preference.

As I mentioned earlier, my first trip to Africa came along rather quickly and I had no time or money to think about a new rifle. I made do with what I had. Not that there was any problem with the rifles I had, there were just a few bumps in the road that I want to bring up. I want to make you aware of them so that when you choose a rifle to take or go to purchase a new one, your ride is a little smoother. The rifles I took were a Remington 700 Classic chambered in .300 Weatherby and a semi-custom 98 Mauser in 8mm as a backup rifle, in case something happened to the Remington. I was unaware of my first bump in the road until after breakfast with Johann that first morning in camp. I pulled my rifles out to show him what I was going to be using for my hunt. If you will remember, my luggage had been misplaced and I had no ammunition, so showing was all I could do at this point. I remember saying that I wanted to hunt with the .300 Wby and, if my luggage did not show up, and asked if we could go back to town and pick up some additional ammunition. He just smiled and said, "nope". Before I could pick my jaw up off the floor, he continued: "There is no way anyone in Otjwarongo would have .300 Weatherby cartridges". He continued, "There is a remote possibility that we could drive back to Windhoek and find some. I would have to make some phone calls to confirm it before I would head back that far." Since it would take us more than eight hours to get there and back, I understood what he meant.

Hint number twenty: bring a rifle chambered in a caliber that is locally available if your ammunition is lost. If I had a .300 Winchester or a 30-06, I could have found cartridges locally. It is relatively easy to check cartridge availability. Just let your PH know what you want to bring and he can tell you whether it is available locally or not. I do not want to scare you away from using your favorite rifle, especially if you shoot it well. Just be aware of the possible consequences. If you are traveling with someone else, you can all but eliminate the problem using **hint number twenty-one: split up each other's ammunition – you take half of your buddies and he takes half of yours.** Of course, both of you could lose your luggage, but probably not.

Next, we looked at my 8mm Mauser. He cycled the bolt and commented that it was a controlled round feed and not a push feed. I said, "Say what?" "The cartridge is picked up by the bolt before it leaves the magazine," he said. I wanted to know what that meant, so he continued his explanation. "A push feed pushes the round from the magazine without grabbing a hold if it.", and "A controlled round feed is less likely to have a round get out of alignment and jam or even dump the round out on the ground by accident." When my luggage showed up a little later, he showed me what he meant. Sure enough, as he cycled the bolt, the round came free from the magazine and it sort of bounced around loose in the breech before the bolt pushed the round into the battery. Completely closing the bolt finally locked it into place. With the controlled round feed as the cartridge slides forward, the rim of the cartridge slides between the bolt face and the extractor. This holds the cartridge securely in place until the bolt is fully closed. What does all of this translate to? Not much, according to some people, and a whole lot according to others. To me, it is just a little extra insurance. Depending on where you are in Africa, every time you round the corner there could be something dangerous looking to make a meal or Silly Putty out of you. If you get overly nervous and hold the rifle at the wrong angle when you cycle the bolt and the cartridge the falls out on the ground, then the trigger pull results in a loud click, you could have problems. Sound a little far-fetched? Maybe, but it has happened, so why take the chance?

With my luggage, and therefore my ammunition, having shown up, we decided to go to the range to check out my equipment. The Remington shot perfectly, but the Mauser was a little off. After looking at it, we decided to take the Remington and go hunting rather than spend more time on the range. We would look at the Mauser after dinner. After dinner, we could find nothing readily identifiable as a problem, and we would try it out tomorrow at lunch. After lunch, the rifle shot worse than the day before. We were baffled. After a few more lunch-time fixes and the rifle continuing to shoot worse and worse, we decided to remount the scope. When Johann tried to loosen the screws that held the scope, he mumbled something and then said he had found the problem. The problem was that the action had not been glass bedded. The lack of bedding in itself was not a major a concern but add the fact that there was a little extra room between the stock and the action, and that was a problem. The fact that I kept the rifle in a climate-controlled vault and now it had been exposed to the very dry African air for four days simply compounded the problem. As a result, the stock had dried out and pulled away from the action enough for it to shift under recoil. It was now effectively useless for the rest of the trip.

When I got home, I took it to my local gunsmith (who, by the way, did not build it to begin with) and had him glass bed it and add through bolts. The fiberglass bedding fills any gaps between the wooden stock and the metal action. The through bolts do exactly what they sound like they are going to do. They pass completely through the stock and action, further locking things into place. The other option I discussed with my gunsmith was using a high-end synthetic stock. It would be less expensive and do the same thing as bedding and through bolts would, and it would never shrink or swell because of the ambient moisture conditions. I thought about it for a few seconds before deciding to stay with wood. The synthetic stock might do the job, but, to me, a gun can be as much a work of art as it is a tool and I just love wood.

The next thing that you should consider is ammunition and, more importantly, the bullet in the ammunition. The bullet should be a premium bullet and should be heavy for caliber. For example, instead of shooting a 150-grain or 165-grain bullet in a 30-06, shoot a 180-grain or 200-grain. The animals in Africa are thicker-skinned and tougher than they are in the United States, and a bullet must hold together and penetrate. There are more and more companies coming out with premium lines of ammunition. Some of the bullets they are using are: Barnes TSX and solids, Trophy Bonded Bear Claw and Sledgehammer, Swift A-frame, Nosler Accubond, Woodleigh, and the list go on. If you have trouble making up your mind, ask your PH what he prefers. After all, he hunts these animals on almost daily basis. He will know what knocks down the animals in a consistent manner. Whatever factory ammunition you choose, do not try to go cheap. Going cheap could cost you a lost animal and possibly ruin your hunt.

If you load your own ammunition, you are sitting in high cotton. You can do just about anything you want to as far as bullet type and (within reason) bullet velocity. Let's talk just a bit about bullet types. There is the expanding bullet that most Americans are familiar with and use in their deer rifles. The expanding bullets for use in Africa are constructed just a little bit tougher to get through the thick hides and large bones of their local critters. These bullets are either solid copper, like the Barnes TSX, or the jackets are bonded to the core like the Nosler Accubond. Bonding the jacket to the core prevents the separation of the bullet's outer jacket from its lead core. The result is deeper penetration and more retained bullet weight. The deeper penetration and more retained weight of these bullets result in more internal damage, and a quicker more humane kill.

The other types of bullets used in Africa are solids. A solid is pretty much what it sounds like – a bullet designed not to mushroom on impact. It is a bullet designed to punch through anything in its way, breaking bone, and penetrating as deeply as possible. Solids see most use on dangerous game, such as in frontal brain shot, for an elephant. Solids are also for follow-up shots for game that does not drop instantly, and very few African game animals drop instantly. The last common use for a solid is if you come across a small trophy game animal and you only have your D.G. rifle. You can use a solid and it makes a nice, neat hole all the way through. This leaves the cape and meat pretty much intact and completely usable.

What these bullets can do is amazing. One day, while out hunting with Johann, we came across a sick eland. We made the decision to put it out of its misery. A shot from my .416 Rigby quickly did just that. I had never fired a .416 solid at anything, so I asked permission to test one on the recently deceased eland. The eland had gone down in somewhat of an upright position. I moved in front of the animal and took aim at its shoulder and fired. We started to look over the animal to see if we saw an exit wound. Johann was standing behind the animal when he muttered an explicative and said, "Look at this".

He then reached down to the base of the tree behind the eland and wiggled my 400-grain Barnes solid out of the tree. That bullet passed through the shoulder bone, through the length of the body, through the tailbone, and into the tree behind it. When I looked at the bullet, the only deformity was from my gun's rifling left when the bullet passed through the barrel. If you are not familiar with the eland, it is the largest member of the antelope family, weighing in excess of 1600 lbs. I would say that the bullet did exactly what it was supposed to do. Unless you have a larger caliber rifle, you will probably not find any factory-loaded solids, but you do need to know about them.

Reloading also allows you to fine tune a load to your specific rifle and practice with reduced velocity loads. The lower powered load will reduce the recoil and be more pleasant to shoot. That should allow you to get in more practice simply because it hurts less to shoot more. Do not practice solely with low power loads. Doing so will cause you problems down the road. First off, the point of impact will be different from your full power hunting loads forcing you to re-sight your rifle. Secondly, the increased recoil of the full power loads will probably make you develop a flinch. If you flinch, you can throw any hope of consistently hitting the target out the window. If you want to use lower powered loads to practice your form and to develop good habits, do so, just switch to full power loads to finish off your training.

If you do not load your own, ask a buddy to do it for you or better yet, have him teach you how to do it. Premium ammunition gets a premium price. You can save yourself a lot of money if you load your own. Even if you have to buy all of the reloading equipment, you can often break even within a few hundred rounds. For example, the current price for a box of factory loaded twenty .416 Rigby that use the same components that I use in my reloads is a little over $200.00. Since I have the brass, I can load the same round for about a $1.50. For my Cape buffalo trip, I went through about one hundred and fifty practice rounds. That is a savings of over $1,200.00, more than enough to pay for the equipment and even buy the brass. The .416 Rigby on the high side of the savings and the savings on other rounds will not be so dramatic, but I would not hesitate to say that if you already have your brass you can load your own for less than thirty-five cents on the dollar.

Reloading also has another couple of advantages. The first is I think it is relaxing and I enjoy the fact that I know what my bullet is going to do when I pull the trigger. For example, I load my .416 to zero at two hundred yards. That puts it at a little less than three inches high at one hundred yards and a little more than ten inches low at three hundred yards. This set up would give me a virtually flat shooting rifle to just over two hundred yards. I knew that the zero at two hundred and three high at one hundred was correct because I verified this at my rifle range. My rifle range is only two hundred yards long, so I was unable to confirm the ten inches at three hundred yards, but I felt that it was correct because I had verified the first two.

It was in Zimbabwe on the last day of the hunt and I still had an impala to take. We spotted a group about halfway across the dry riverbed of the Sengwa River. Phil and I had a long belly crawl to get to some bush at the edge of the riverbed. When we finally got there, the antelope had moved off to approximately two hundred and twenty-five yards. I was having trouble picking out the ram Phil wanted me to take due to the waving grass that was concealing us at the river's edge, and because the herd was constantly milling about. By the time we were both looking at the same animal, the herd had moved to just over three hundred yards away. Phil asked if I still wanted to take the shot. I told him I did if he was sure about the distance. Phil said he was sure because he knew the river. I felt good about my position. As I was sitting and the hunting sticks were stretched out low in front of me, the rifle felt rock solid. I picked the spot on the ram that I wanted to hit, moved up the backside of its neck to a point that I estimated to be ten inches above it. I took a deep breath, let half of it out, and squeezed the trigger. The r e c o i l

My antelope taken at just over 300 yards with my .416 Rigby

The riverbed I shot across to get my antelope

of the .416 took me off the sticks and I lost sight of the ram. Before I could find it again in the scope, Phil was slapping me on the back saying "good shot", and then asking me to clear my rifle. Before I let the shot sound too good, I have to admit that I forgot to allow for wind drift, and the bullet struck further back than I had intended. The drop was exactly what I thought it was going to be, but, instead of passing through both shoulders, the bullet had broken the spine of the impala and dropped him where he stood. I am not telling this story to impress you with my shooting. I am telling the story to impress upon you two important points, not just for Africa, but for hunting anywhere else as well. The first is that if you learn to hand load your own ammunition, you can fine-tune your load so that you know exactly what it is capable of doing. Next, and more importantly, you must know your rifle. To know your rifle, you must shoot and shoot often.

The last little thing I want to talk about in regards to ammunition is the current trend that requires all ammunition to be in a locked box inside your luggage. I sort of understand the logic behind this new regulation, but I think it is unnecessary. Regardless of what I think, it is a regulation and if you take ammunition to Africa, you have to deal with it. At the current time, it does not matter what the boxes are made of, just that they are lockable. With the weight restrictions placed on you by the airlines, you need to keep weight to a minimum. I looked at steel cash boxes, but they weighed too much, and fishing tackle boxes were too big. What I finally decided to use were the plastic boxes for storing and transporting pistols. If you take the foam out of one side, you can put two to four, twenty round ammo boxes in them. Add a small combination lock and you have a storage system that weighs about a pound and costs less than ten dollars. When you get back home, you can turn it right back into a pistol box.

Some airlines have a written policy that ammunition must be in its original container, for what reason I do not know. As you might guess, I am normally short on factory boxes because I buy components and make my own cartridges. I store my cartridges in the translucent plastic ammunition boxes. I like the ability to see how many rounds are left without having to open the box. Technically, I should not be allowed to fly with them, but I have never had a problem. The reason I mention this is to give you some time to save up some of the factory boxes if you would like to do so.

Let's take a look at another controversial subject: optics. There are lots of good optic manufacturers out there, and I am not going to take sides either for or against. I am just going to give you a few things to think about. There are scopes that start at $50.00 and scopes that cost over $2400.00, and anything in-between. The only thing I want to say about this is "Do Not Go Cheap". Buy the best you can afford. You are going on a hunt that costs thousands of dollars. Do not take a chance on ruining it with a cheap scope. I once thought that just because I had a scope with a lifetime warranty, I had a good scope. That makes sense doesn't it? Let me tell you what I learned the hard way.

It was my first trip to Namibia, and my hunt was going well. I had my kudu, my warthog, and my steinbuck. I had two days left and I was on the trail of a gemsbok. We were up on top of a kopje or a good-sized hill when Johann spotted some that we needed a closer look at. We eased down the rocky side of the kopje until we were about one hundred and fifty yards away, and thirty to forty yards above them. Johann picked one for me to take and I used a boulder for a rifle rest and pulled the trigger. The gemsbok staggered for a second then just sat down. Being my first time in Africa, I did not know to keep shooting until it was all the way dead. I just kept my eye on it and waited for it to fall over. Well, instead of falling over, it got up and ran off. I never had time to even think about a second shot. We walked over to the original spot and found only one little drop of blood and then no more. We tracked for a while only catching glimpses of a gemsbok running away from us some eight hundred yards in front of us. Johann decided not to push it anymore and suggested we go back to camp for lunch. While we were eating, he had another idea – "Let's check your scope".

After we finished eating, we went back to the range and I fired two shots. They were dead-center, but twelve inches high. That would put my shot at the gemsbok eighteen inches high. My shot probably just grazed the back of his head and stunned him for a moment. When he got his bell un-rung, he just got the heck out of dodge. What does all of this have to do with a lifetime warranty on a scope? After scratching our heads trying to figure out how the scope got off, I made a comment to the effect that all was going to be ok. In that the scope had a lifetime warranty and I would send it back when I got home. Johann grinned and told me that a lifetime warranty meant nothing in the African bush, and that when I was back home with a replaced or fixed scope, I would not have any gemsbok to look at it with. He also reminded me that since I had wounded the gemsbok and if we could not find it later, I still had a trophy fee to pay. I kept that scope for a long time to remind me of the lesson that I learned that day.

Ok, what do you look for in a scope? Let's start with the glass. There are coated lenses, and multicoated lenses. What you are looking for are fully multi-coated lenses. Fully multi-coated lenses have multiple layers of coating on all glass surfaces. The coating helps with light transmission. The more coating, the more light that is transmitted through the scope and the brighter the image is. The next thing I would look for is a scope purged of oxygen by the use of a gas such as nitrogen. If you push all of the oxygen out, the moisture goes with it. Without any trapped moisture, the lenses cannot fog up. This could be a problem since the daily temperature range is so wide.

The next logical question would be about magnification. It is just a personal opinion, but a variable-power 3x9 will do just about anything you need it to in Africa. A shot over two hundred yards is the exception rather than the rule, with most of my shots coming under one hundred yards. My personal exception to a 3x9 scope is on a dangerous game rifle. I currently use a variable 1.5 x 5 powered scope. The field of view is more important than magnification on a D.G. rifle, especially if something that wants you dead is coming at you hard and fast. If your scope is turned to a high magnification, you may not be able to get what is coming at you in the crosshairs before it is too late. **Hint number twenty-two: if you are in a dangerous game area, unless your PH tells you differently, leave your scope on its lowest power.** This simple thing could save your bacon if something big and mean makes its presence known form a short distance away. When you find the animal you are looking for then you can turn your scope to whatever power you want. Personally, I like to get on the shooting sticks, find my quarry, and then turn the magnification up if I need to before taking the shot.

The last topic on scopes is the reticle. On a plains game rifle, use whatever you prefer or what is already on your hunting rifle. If you are going to buy a new scope and are open to new ideas, let me run one by you. Look at a German #4 reticle. I had never seen one before Africa and I like them so much I am switching out my hunting scopes with crosshairs to a German #4 reticle. A German # 4 reticle is a heavy set of crosshairs with the top half of the vertical post gone. The other difference is there is a dot in the center instead of an x formed by the crosshairs. I find this reticle gives me very quick target acquisition and then onto the vitals even quicker. Without the top part of the post, I can see the animal as a whole much easier, and that makes holding on the animals vitals much easier. I would also recommend the German # 4 for a dangerous game scope because of its quick target acquisition. Whichever reticle you use on a dangerous game rifle, it should be quick on target. In other words, it should draw your eye to the center of the scope and then onto the target. The reason I do not like crosshairs for dangerous game is I take too long for me to center the scope on the target. I end up moving the scope up and down, and then side to side, before I can settle in on the sweet spot. One other thing, and this is a personal taste kind of thing, but my aging eyes really like a lighted reticle in low-light situations. Not the whole crosshairs, mind you, just a center dot. That illuminated dot on the dark shape of a game animal in low light makes it easy for me to hold steady on the animal's sweet spot.

One scope accessory that you really need to take is a cover that can keep the majority of the dust out. The dust is very fine and gets into everything. I have tried the flip-up type of scope covers and the type that fits over the whole scope. Both types will do the job but each has its own disadvantage as well. I have tried everything but glue to keep the flip-up type on my Safari rifles, but the heavy recoil always makes them fall off at the most inopportune times. It is just a personal thing, but I do not want to attach them permanently to the scope. I know that as soon as I put them on permanently, something will break or I'll have to take them off for some other reason, and then I'll be forced to say something I'll regret later. These also will not work if you have to turn the whole eyepiece on your scope to change magnification.

The type that fits over the whole scope has its problems as well. First off, and probably due to user error, they cannot seem to stay where I put them when they are not on the scope. Secondly, the rubber ones can trap moisture and allow it to condense on the exterior lens surface. The cloth ones allow moisture to escape, but allow some of the fine dust to get through. Make your own decision, but take one or the other. I can tell you from experience that mounting your rifle and seeing only a fuzzy, dirty picture through your scope can also make you say something you will regret later.

I want to add a brief word or two about scope rings. This is more for the large-caliber or magnum rifles, which, to me, is anything with more that twenty-eight to thirty foot pounds of recoil. Use only steel rings and bases. The recoil coming off these rifles can be punishing to your scope mounts. -Make sure that your mounts can take it. I also recommend the use of "Loctite" or something like it to make sure your screws cannot come loose or back out. If you have a rifle with iron sights, which I highly recommend on a dangerous game rifle, consider quick detachable mounts. The mounts made today go back to your zero and are very durable. The reason I suggest quick detachable mounts revolves around dangerous game in thick cover. If I have to follow up wounded dangerous game in the thick brush, I absolutely do not want a scope.

I want to be able to put the rifle against my shoulder and get off the first shot in a matter of two or three seconds. If a buffalo or leopard is waiting in ambush, two or three seconds might be all the time you have. Your eye simply cannot find the target through a scope near as quickly as it can with iron sights. With the detachable system, you can take your scope off and put your scope in your pocket or pack in less than a minute. Then you can follow up the wounded animal in the most prepared state possible.

Let me see if I can give a brief summation of the first part on this chapter by telling you what I did after getting back from my first Safari.

The bad news about this is I had become hopelessly hooked on Africa and knew I would be going back. The good news is I got two new rifles to go back with. Johann had given me a starting point by recommending CZ rifles. After I did my own research and looked at several custom gunsmiths, I went with the CZ "Safari Classic", which can be custom built to your specifications. After a few trips to my local gun shop, I started dealing directly with Jason Morton of CZ USA. He asked me the right questions, listened to my request, and then told me whether my ideas made sense or not. CZ built the rifles for me and a short time later, I was blasting away.

What did I choose? Let me tell you. For my plains-game rifle, I chose a 9.3x62 Mauser and, for my dangerous game rifle, I chose a .416 Rigby. I chose these calibers because they are available just about everywhere in Africa and they are both classic safari calibers. Otto Bock, a German rifle maker, introduced the 9.3 in 1905. He wanted to give the farmers in the German colonies a cartridge that was economical compared to the English cartridges and that was capable of dealing with African-sized game. John Rigby introduced the .416 Rigby in 1911 for his magnum line of sporting rifles. The .416 Rigby went on to become one of the most highly respected and successful calibers to ever be used in Africa. There are a few others that might give it a run for its money, but not many.

Both rifles were built exactly alike so I could switch from one to the other without having to re-familiarize myself with the rifle. Each rifle had three leaf folding rear sights and a hooded front sight. I added barrel bands to give me more room with the sling and they are on traditional safari rifles. I also happen to think that they look cool. Both had a jeweled bolt and a custom worked actions. Each action was glass bedded and had two through bolts. I went to deluxe wood, so I got positively gorgeous rifles. The only difference between the two was the .416 got a little longer barrel to make use of all of the powder in the cartridge and to help with recoil. I also had CZ add a mercury recoil reducer in the .416. As a result, neither rifle beats my shoulder to death. I added "Warne Quick Detach" scope rings and a 3x9 "Burris Euro Diamond" scope on the 9.3x62, and a "Leupold VX3 1.5x5 on the .416, both with a German #4 lighted reticle. I have been extremely happy with both rifles and they have never failed me. I wish you as much good luck as I had in choosing your rifles.

I know that I am going to get in trouble for saying this, but I am going to anyway. Unless you are used to carrying and shooting with binoculars, they are a waste of weight coming over on the airplane. In addition, unless you are an old hand at scoring the African trophy, you are going to be relying on your PH to tell you which one to shoot. If you want to look at the game before you start a stalk, you can see it through your scope just as easy as a pair of binoculars. If you want to use your binoculars to spot game, good luck. The shape and coloring of most African came are unfamiliar to us and, therefore, are hard to spot. I gave up trying to spot game from a distance a long time ago. I can be on top of a kopje looking in the same area as Johann, with the same binocular he has, and still not see the animals he does. In all the days I have spent hunting with him, I think I have seen one animal before he has. This fact has prompted me to leave my full size binoculars at home. I may carry a compact set in one of the leg pockets of my hunting pants but not always. I have learned to trust him to put me on the kind of game I want to hunt and, therefore, I do not need to carry the extra weight. With that said, feel free to take a pair of binoculars if you like, but do not be surprised if you find yourself leaving them back at camp or in the hunting truck.

Protecting your guns on the way to Africa is not necessarily an easy task. Most airlines appear to have top-secret special training facilities just to teach baggage handlers how to damage, damage proof luggage. One of my gun cases has two locking rods, one on each side that secure the case in the closed position. On my last trip home, one of the locking rods was ripped loose from the case without tearing out the holes it was threaded through or breaking the lock that held it in place. I still have not figured out how they did that. My point in all of this is: do not use just any old hard case to transport your guns. I have two, one composite four-gun case and an aluminum two-gun case. Both cases weigh the same and both of them have wheels. The wheels have the advantage of letting you pull the case through an airport, but the wheels will not allow the case to stand on its end even if you are holding it. I bought the composite four-gun case first, figuring that if I wanted to take more than two guns, I could. The problem is, with that the weight of the case and my two rifles, I am at the weight limit set by the airline. For me to take an extra gun I would have to pay an overweight fee. I could pay the extra fee, I guess, but so far, I have wanted not to spend the money more than I wanted to take an extra gun. This case locks all four latches with a key.

The only problem with the locks is that they are not TSA (Transportation Security Administration) locks, meaning that, if I am not around and the Transportation Security Authority or any other countries officials want in it, the locks will most likely be broken and render the case useless. The metal case I bought just because it has a flip-out shelf that turns it into a hand truck and I could use TSA locks on it. Strapping your carry-on or other bag to this shelf is very handy for getting through the airport. Undoing the strap that holds the shelf up, and then your luggage to the shelf, is a problem. It takes way too long to take the shelf down and then secure it back in the unused position. I need to sit down and figure out an easier way to do that someday. The fact I can use TSA locks is comforting to me, because the thought of my guns bouncing around an airport in an unlocked case scares the dickens out of me. The size of the case and its material is purely up to you. I would offer two pieces of advice. The first is to make sure that built-in locks are TSA locks or you can furnish your own TSA locks. The second is to find a reference or review of the case you plan to buy. It can be an online review or a reference from someone who has one, but do your homework. One last thought about gun cases – there is a good possibility that you will need a soft to protect your rifle in the hunting truck. They are a pain to pack, so check with your PH, and ask him if you need to bring one. There is one more type of gun case that I should mention, and that is the one that looks like a hard case for a golf bag. With this type of case you use your clothing to pad your gun. While I have never used one I can certainly see the utility of using this type.

The last two physical items to discuss in the hunting tools category have to do with cleaning and maintaining your gun. Since space and weight are an issue with hunting abroad. I would suggest using either "BoreSnake" or the "Otis Technologies" cleaning kit. The Otis Kit probably cleans more thoroughly, but it has what could possibly considered as a flammable liquid by an overzealous official. Even though it should not be a problem, the confusion could cause you unneeded stress and delays at the airport. With that in mind, I lean toward the BoreSnake. You should not need a heavy cleaning anyway. I just used mine for a quick pass after checking the scope at the range. The second item is a small gun-smithing screwdriver kit. The kind I am talking about are the ones with the one handle and multiple bits. You can find them in the ten to fifteen dollar range. In the case of loose screws, or if you have field strip your gun, they can be invaluable. If you want to make room to bring back something else, they make a great thank you for your PH. Better yet, buy a little nicer set and plan on leaving it.

My last section in this chapter has to do with your preparation / practice to hunt in Africa. The first thing I want to bring up is shooting sticks. There is a 99.99953 percent probability you will be using a set in Africa. **Hint number twenty-three: buy a set of three legged shooting sticks, and shoot at least two hundred rounds from them.** Two hundred rounds might sound like a lot of practice, but I consider it a minimum. Shooting off a three-legged tripod might not sound that difficult and it is not. It is foreign and different from any shooting you have ever done before. Practice, however, makes perfect in this situation and I will tell you how to do it while having a bit of fun.

Before I get into the practice routine, I want to give you my next hint and it is a good one. **Hint number twenty-four: if you do not already have one get a scoped twenty-two caliber rifle with the same action as the rifle you are going to use in Africa get one**. I even went so far as to have CZ make a .22 to match my Safari rifles, and I consider that one of my best decisions ever. It allowed me to practice my technique without beating up my shoulder and without spending a small fortune in ammunition. By shooting the .22, I was able to put over seven hundred practice rounds down range to prepare for my last safari.

I first had to beef up my backstop because of the .416. I made my backstop by stacking a wall of logs that is four feet thick, six feet tall and ten feet wide. I used logs, but you can use whatever you have to make it as big as you can. The logs actually facilitated my use of targets. I drove nails an inch or so into the logs at random spots around the periphery of the backstop, leaving enough room in the center to place one regular paper target. To start a session I would blow up balloons and tie them off, leaving enough of the balloon behind the knot to force over the head of the nail. I then took aluminum cans and skeet and sat them on the logs in between the balloons. When I was finished, I had created my own shooting arcade.

I started shooting at fifty yards with the "safari grade" .22. My practice routine consisted of shooting five rounds in the following manor. With the shooting sticks set up in front of me, I would pick out a target, bring the rifle to my shoulder, get on the shooting sticks, center the target, and then pull the trigger. When the target broke, I quickly cycled the bolt and moved to the next target. When I cycled the bolt, I stayed on the sticks, kept the rifle against my shoulder and cheek, and kept my sight picture. When I moved from one target to the next, I could almost simulate an initial hit on a game animal and then follow up shots.

On my first trip to Africa, Johann told me that my shooting had the typical American shooting flaw. When I asked for an explanation, he told me that after their initial shot most Americans tended to sit back, admire their shot, and wait for the animal to fall down. He followed up by telling me that if I did that too often in Africa, I would start to lose some of my animals. It took losing the gemsbok that I told you about earlier to drive that point home. **Hint number twenty-five: practice getting ready for a quick follow-up shot**. That sounds easier that it is. It took me more than just a few times to be able to stay in position and on target while I worked the bolt. Shooting the .22 made a world of difference in my practice sessions while learning to do this. The light recoil allowed me to focus on technique without worrying about being pounded every time the gun went off.

Before I go any further with the practice session, I want to give you **hint number twenty-six: when mounting a rifle with a scope, keep both eyes open until you see the target through the scope, and then close one eye (preferably not the one behind the scope)**. This also takes some getting used to, but I promise that if you turn town the scopes power and keep both eyes open, you will get on target quicker and get more shots. By closing one eye when you shoulder your rifle, you lose more than fifty percent of your sight picture, and I guarantee that is not a good thing.

After I became proficient at fifty yards, I moved back to one hundred and started all over again. By the way, my definition of proficient when using the .22 was five shots and five hits in less than twenty five seconds. If I got bored standing behind the sticks, I would practice off hand or sitting. If your schedule allows it, practice at different times of the day. It helps to break up your routine, and varying the amount of light and conditions simulates hunting better. If you have quick detachable scope rings practice taking them off and shooting with your iron sights. I would practice this at fifty yards or so, but I would take a few shots from a little closer and a little further away. Shoot enough to be certain that you know where your iron sights will put the bullet in a consistent manner. Taking the scope off to use your iron sights will also give you practice with the release mechanism. It will also give you confidence that your scope will return to zero if you do your part and put it back on correctly. I probably spent three weeks with the .22 before I even took the 9.3 or .416 to the range and, even when I did finally take them, I always had a practice round or two with the .22 before using the other rifles. If I started flinching or getting frustrated, I could just break out the .22 and get myself back under control. By starting out and getting plenty of practice with the .22, I got my form in shape. With my form what it should be, the large rifles did not seem to kick quite so badly. With

My three rifles, built as close to exactly alike as possible

the large rifles not kicking so badly, I got more practice in. With more practice, the better shot I became, and I did it all while having fun. Get the picture? Shooting your hunting rifles with full-powered hunting loads is very, very important to a successful hunt. Having fun while you practice is the surest way to make you practice a lot. Before I left on my last trip, I had put close to two hundred rounds through my 9.3 and about one hundred and fifty rounds through my .416.

There is one more aspect of practice that no one likes, but it is necessary. The first one is practice shooting while winded. Pretend that you have just seen a new Safari Club International record-book kudu disappear over a hill a few hundred yards away. The sun has set and there is not much shooting light left. If you run to the crest of the hill, you just might get a shot at him. You make the jog to the hilltop and see the kudu seventy yards away, head down and feeding. You get him your scope only to realize that your scope is going up and down like a kid on a trampoline. Can you get your breathing under control and make a shot before the light fades or the kudu walks off? With practice, you normally can get your breathing under control in short order, even if you are not in the best of shape. Being in good shape helps, but practicing breath control while you are winded helps even more. For me, I have to take a few seconds and a few extra deep breaths before I think about the shot. While I am taking my deep breaths, I am locating my target and getting it in my scope. After I accomplish this, and while keeping my eye on my target, I start to monitor my breathing. As soon as I can let that half a breath out, and hold it for a second, I am ready to shoot. By getting yourself into position and getting your sight picture lined up while your breathing is recovering, you are doing two things at once, saving time and allowing you to get off a shot more quickly.

To practice shooting winded try this: instead of just a brisk walk or short run to get you winded, try what I call the "tortured hunter sprint". While there is often cover of some kind in the bushveld at some point I can guarantee you that your PH will put you into a stooped-over crouch and then ask you to cover ground quickly. If you are a young buck without a slightly widening middle, that may not be a problem. For those of us who do not resemble that last remark it could be a problem. My advice is to practice bending over, squatting down, holding your gun in one hand, and then walking very fast. Doing this will get you in shape and let you practice shooting while you are breathing hard. It also has the added benefit of giving you the much-needed practice of unfolding yourself after making such a sprint. I say this sort of tongue and cheek, but I am serious when I say this is a good way to practice.

CHAPTER SEVEN
Camp Life

I do not really know where to begin when I describe camp life. Should I start with the type of accommodations? Should it be the food or the social atmosphere? Camp is all of these and a lot more. Aside from the animals and the hunt, it is the embodiment of an African safari. Can I do it justice? Probably not, but I'll try my best. When I first started thinking safari camp, I was thinking tent camp. The only knowledge that I had came from others. The others came from a different time, a time that went from before the turn of the last century to just a few decades ago. They were Pete Hathaway Capstick, Robert Ruark, Theodore Roosevelt, and Frederick Courteney Selous, just to name a few. Reading their works had predisposed me to a tent camp. I wanted to be like the people that I had read about. If I just could put myself in their shoes I could possibly have as grand adventures as they had. Just maybe I could, it was worth a try anyway. They all had tent camps so that is where I will start.

The tent camps of today are not really like the ones of yesteryear; they are a lot nicer. In the old days, people on safari used tents to facilitate mobility. The safari used to break camp every day or every few days to change hunting locations and find fresh game. With the speed and ease at which we can move between hunting areas with our modern hunting vehicles, it makes moving the whole camp unnecessary. We can travel many miles away from camp hunt all day and still be home for dinner. What the tents are absolutely necessary for is ambiance – the sound the material makes while flapping in the breeze or the sound the zipper makes when you step out into the predawn to start your hunt. The tent also allows you to hear all of the sounds of the African night and it reminds you that only a piece of canvas separates you from those noises.

All of the romanticism aside, modern tent camps are just that modern. Mine was on a concrete slab with an en-suite toilet and shower. The slab

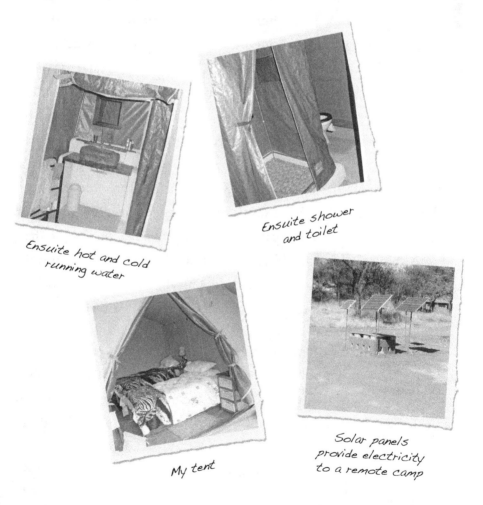

Ensuite hot and cold running water

Ensuite shower and toilet

My tent

Solar panels provide electricity to a remote camp

One of the chalets built right into the hillside

helped keep creepy crawlies out and gave the tent a smooth floor. There were two single beds, with a nightstand for each. There were electric lights and two modern versions of a wardrobe. There were just about all of the conveniences of home. Just in case you were wondering, yes, they are still hot in the afternoon sun and downright cold at night. A tent camp could have a dining tent or an open dining cover. Either will work and preserve the atmosphere that a tent camp projects. Today's modern tent camps offer you the best of both worlds, an old-time safari setting with a luxury that the first timers on safari could not imagine.

If you would like to feel a little more secure (from the noises of the night), staying in a chalet may be more to your liking. I have stayed in two different camps with chalets, Tualuka and Ingwe, and both were very comfortable and very different. The first place I stayed was Tualuka. It had a

The view from my chalet

huge main lodge that encompassed a multi-level dining and sitting area, and separate levels for the bar and lounging area. The walls were masonry and the floors tile. Its roof consisted of huge post and beams, which held up the thatched roof. The leather-covered furniture was more than comfortable. To sit on it even for a short time invited a nap. Even though the structure was open on three sides, it was remarkably cool during the heat of the day. The guest chalets were miniature versions of the main lodge. Each chalet was slightly different from the other but they each had

Tualuka Safari Lodge

The dining area in the main lodge

a sitting area, a separate dressing area, bath area, and private porch. Due to the masonry construction, thatched roof, and closable windows and doors, the chalets are remarkably well insulated. This is particularly nice if you wanted to escape the mid-day heat. With the outside temperature in the mid-to-upper eighties, the inside temperature is often in the low seventies. The chalets were even more ornate than the lodges. The interior doors were handmade and custom carved with African wildlife. Some of the interior furniture was hand-carved as well. One of the neatest things about the individual chalets and the lodge is that are built into the side of a kopje, making use of the boulders and natural stone inside each unit. This is truly five-star lodging in the middle of the African bush.

The other camp, Ingwe, had chalets that were remarkably nice considering its remote location. It was far inside a national park. It, too, consisted of masonry walls with a thatched roof, and private porch. The level of trim was more in line with the remoteness of the camp. It was very functional, clean, and secure. It was also very nice to have the extra room versus a tent. The more-than-ample floor and dresser space allowed me to spread my gear out for easy access. All of the camps I have been in are extremely comfortable and functional. Take your pick; I am sure that anything you pick will be to your liking. Just remember what I said in Chapter Three, "Picking your Team". Tell your booking agent what you want and expect, and that should remove any chance at being disappointed.

I cannot say enough good things about the food served on safari. The food at Tualuka rivals or exceeds the best I have had anywhere. The food at Ingwe was also excellent. It does not matter if you are in a tent camp or luxury chalet camp; the food quality is always superb and there is normally more than you could possibly eat. While the daily menus will vary, lunch and dinner are usually centered around wild game. It could be game that you shot, but, more than likely, it will be game taken by a previous hunter. Using the previous hunter's game allows the staff to age it to perfection before it is prepared for the table. If you are a "meat and potatoes" type of person, you will think that you have died and gone to Heaven. If not, and you have let the camp know what you like, and, if it is available to the camp, it will be there. **Hint number twenty-seven: let your safari operator know your food preferences; more importantly, let them know your food restrictions, such as food allergies.** Even if your allergy is a minor one, it is best to avoid an attack if possible. You certainly do not want to risk an anaphylaxis type reaction in the bush. If a severe food reaction is possible and you travel with an epinephrine pen, make sure your PH knows about it and how to use it if necessary.

Breakfast will be well before first light, but, before I get to breakfast, I want to give you the next hint. **Hint number twenty-eight: bring an old-fashioned windup alarm clock and get yourself up and to breakfast on time. Your PH or camp staff member will appreciate this. It keeps them from having to get up extra early in order to wake you up, and from having to wait on you to get ready for breakfast.** A typical breakfast could be hot or cold. A hot breakfast could consist of bacon, sausage, and eggs or oatmeal. A typical cold breakfast might be sliced cold cuts and bread or cereal and yogurt. I used to combine the most wonderful type of granola cereal with hot milk for the best of both worlds. It was quick and easy for my host and it lasted me until lunch. Add a couple of mugs of hot coffee or tea and you are set for the morning. If possible, I like to take a cup of coffee with me when I head out in the morning. I enjoy sipping it as I travel to where I am going and, to be honest, it helps ward off the morning chill. If this sounds like you, the next hint is one you will want to remember. **Hint number twenty-nine is taking a travel mug with a closeable lid with you.** I have not seen one in a camp yet, and using a regular coffee cup while riding through the bushveld is going to get you burnt, wet, or both. Since you will be leaving camp before daylight, a cup of coffee to go is a nice way to ease into the day.

What's for lunch will depend upon whether or not you are going to be back at camp or dining a-la-bush. If you are in camp, there is no telling what goodies you might find, but it will probably be on the light side. I have had everything from hamburgers made from eland, served with fresh homemade rolls, to salad, fruit, and cheese. Lunch in the bush will be similarly light and more like a picnic. There could be cold francolin or sand grouse served with potato salad and bread or last night's leftover roast served cold with cheese and chutney. With all of this good food, it is difficult not to eat your fill, and then some, but I recommend against it.

After lunch, you will probably get a chance for something I do recommend, which is **hint number thirty: take an afternoon nap if possible.** Most of the game you will be hunting will be in the shade somewhere during the heat of the day and I suggest you do the same. If you are in camp for lunch, you will find that it is a very laid-back time of day. After lunch is over and things are put away, camp will pretty much shut down. There will be a few people moving about, but the majority will be enjoying their afternoon nap. If you are the type that cannot take a siesta, be considerate of the others. A nap is part of their everyday routine. There is a lot of activity that goes on in camp before you get up and after you go to bed, so a nap maybe more of a necessity than a luxury. In camp, a nap is easy, just head back to your nice comfortable bed. On most occasions when I have done this, I was asleep before I got my eyes all the way closed. Most people will have no problem drifting off to sleep for a short time. Just remember to set your alarm clock before lying down. If you do have trouble taking a nap, find something to read or study your shot placement book, clean your equipment, or anything that is quiet and you can do by yourself. Your PH and camp staff would oblige you if you had to have someone entertain you, but I promise you that they would really appreciate the down time.

If you are still in the bush, a proper nap takes a little more effort. First, you have to find a suitable location. There are three requirements for a good napping site. The first is shade. The location you choose must provide shade now and keep providing shade as the sun moves across the sky. Allowing for shade shifting was another lesson I learned the hard way when I woke up sweaty and sunburned after my shade disappeared. The second factor in a proper nap spot is the absence of rocks where you plan to lay your slumbering body down. The last thing to think about is to make sure there is no insect life in the same shade that you plan to occupy. Waking up with a bunch of creepy crawlies between you and your clothing is not something I would like to experience. A proper nap will recharge your batteries enough to have a good afternoon hunting. If you have to follow up a wounded animal, and the track is long, it may be well after dark when you get back to the hunting truck and eventually back to camp.

The time when I get back to camp and the day's hunt is over is my favorite time on safari. It is the magical time of the African sunset. Do not get me wrong, the sunrises can be spectacular, but I love the sunsets. Let me take you there with me. Try to imagine yourself there as I describe the evening. The sky turns the most wonderful shades of blue, and the shadows seem to move across the ground on their own. The temperature drops quickly and you shiver while you change from your hunting clothes into your camp attire. Next, you catch that first smell of smoke coming off the fire and it draws you closer as the only source of heat available. Waiting close to the fire is your host with your favorite beverage. A "sundowner" – that is what the locals call it. It is more than just having a drink; it is about winding up the day and winding you down. You pull your chair up to the fire, enjoy a smoke if you like, and lots of great conversation. If there is more than one hunter in your group, you can relive each other's adventures of the day. Old stories are retold and all becomes right with the world, or at least this little corner of it. As the story swapping comes to an end, and the liquid from your last refill works its way toward the bottom of your glass, your nose may catch a whiff of the delights to come. A few minutes later, the call will come to assemble for dinner, and, as you make your way toward the table, your senses are completely overwhelmed. Here in the deepest, darkest, Africa is a table set with fine china and crystal. There are decanters of fine wine, bowls of steaming vegetables, and a platter of roasted beast. The sight forces you to concentrate on not drooling down your shirt and embarrassing yourself. As you look around the table, you realize that you are not alone in your plight, as everyone in attendance seems to be having the same problem. When everyone takes a seat, a short blessing is asked, and the feast begins. The conversation magically ceases for the first few minutes of dinner as everyone enjoys each bite. Just as you finally convince your mouth to stop taking in any more food, your sense of smell is assaulted once more by (what else?) dessert. Pastries, pies, puddings, or cake, what would it be tonight? All of this food will ruin even the most staunch dieter's resolve. After everyone has had to loosen his or her belt a notch or two, it is back to the fire with one last glass of wine. For those that enjoy a good cigar, I cannot think of a better time or place to enjoy a smoke. The conversation soon turns to which quarry you are searching and then to coming up with a game plan for tomorrow. Once again, the conversation starts to lag. Others start to excuse themselves and head off to bed, and you fight the urge to follow. There is something about sitting around the fire watching the flames dance while enjoying the serenade provided courtesy of the African night. It is easy to think back fifty or a hundred years and imagine what it was like then. It was probably not too much different from what you are

Sundowners photo by Phillip Smythe

Africa just after sunset

The most relaxing place for your sundowner

experiencing tonight. You wonder what the hunters that came before you talked about. Were they hunting elephant, lion, plains game, or the same as you? Soon the realization that you cannot resist the call of your warm, comfortable bed any longer works its way into your conscious thought. As you stand and force one foot in front and head toward your quarters, you feel the cold of the night wrap itself around you. You are barely able to get your things ready for tomorrow as sleep comes for you. As you drift off, a thought comes to you and you smile as you realize that you get to do this all again tomorrow.

The description I just gave will sound a little farfetched until you experience it for the first time. Then, and only then, you will know beyond all doubt that that I said is true. The game prepared rivals the finest beef that I have ever eaten. As matter of fact, the best steak that I have ever had was gemsbok. A close second is a butterflied zebra steak filled with a cream sauce and feta cheese. Freshly made bread and vegetables or salad will round out the menu and nutritionally balance the meal for those of us that care about such things. The desserts really are sinfully wonderful concoctions that I can't seem to say no to. Now that I have told you all this, I need to make you aware of **hint number thirty-one: do yourself a favor, diet before going to Africa, because you will gain weight there.**

Most camps have a very dedicated staff. They want you to have the best time possible and will do whatever it takes (within reason) to make your stay a memorable one. The quantity of staff will vary from place to place and what you are hunting could slightly affect the number as well. The staff quantity and positions should loosely resemble the following. As you might gather from the preceding paragraphs most camps have an outstanding cook. In addition to the cook, there will be someone to help the cook and then to serve and clear the table. There will be a housekeeper or cleaning person. This person may also have the responsibility of doing the laundry as well, or the camp may be sufficiently large as to have a full time laundry person. The laundry person will be of great use to you while you are in camp. Since you have only a limited number of clothing items, plan to leave something to be laundered each day. You may as well make use of it, as there will be laundry done in camp every day.

When I took my buffalo in Zimbabwe, there were only four of us to get the large animal in the bed of the truck. Their solution was to cut the animal in half. That worked out well and we got it into the truck with a minimum of grunting and groaning. I thought this was really cool until I looked down at myself and discovered I was coated from my chest to my toes in blood. I figured the clothes had had it, but, to my amazement, they came back cleaned and pressed the next morning.

Housekeeping will clean your room and make your bed each day. They will also return to turn down your bed every night. Do both of you a favor and keep your room neat. If you leave stuff strewn all over everything, and they come in to straighten and clean, things may not get placed where you think they should go. I am not saying that things will be taken. What I am saying is, remember how your spouse can put things away and they are hard to find? You do not want to spend your vacation looking for something that you should have put away yourself. There will also be a groundskeeper and/or a maintenance man. They are responsible for keeping the grounds manicured and in good general condition. In addition to your PH, there will be at least one tracker. There is also someone designated as the camp skinner and butcher. This person will be responsible for the preparation of your trophies cape and trophy care. Why would you need to know all this? There are three reasons. The first is these people are there to make sure you have a great time. Secondly if there is a problem or something unexpected pops up, you need to let someone know. There will be someone in camp capable of handling just about anything that comes up. The last reason is the "tip" of the staff that you need to leave at the end of the hunt. I have never gotten a straight answer when I have asked about "tipping", but I'll try to give you a straight answer in a later chapter. Right now, I just want you to be aware of how many staff members there are and how they can help you.

After the evening hunt comes the time that almost anyone who has ever dreamed of taking a safari has heard about. It is time for the African "happy hour" or a sundowner. Whether you prefer an alcoholic beverage, fruit juice, or soda, this time of day will, no doubt, soon become a favorite. If you are part of a group, this may be the first time during the day that you will have a chance to catch up and talk with everyone else. It is time for stories and laughter, practical jokes or just about any social activity you can think of. With the departure of the sun, the temperature will drop as well and the lighting of the fire will be a welcome sight. Soon everyone is standing next to the flames rubbing their hands together and getting warm. A short while later, most everyone has kicked back with his or her feet up in front of the fire, resting and relaxing. During sundowners is when you would be introduced to any dinner guest that may have arrived. This could be anyone from family members to the safari company management, or perhaps even the owner. It is a nice way to get to know someone casually before dinner. The main thing to remember about sundowner time is to have fun and relax. The only suggestion I will make about your choice of drink for a sundowner is **hint number thirty-two: if you like to have wine with certain things at dinner, check the menu before ordering your cocktail for a sundowner.** Switching to red wine after several rounds of bourbon or brandy could lead to suffering from FHS the following morning. FHS or "Fat Head Syndrome" has been the scourge of hunters on safari for as long as there have been safaris. Just about any activity that is associated with hunting will antagonize all of the symptoms of FHS. I recommend avoiding it at all cost. Have fun, but not too much fun, if you know what I mean.

This section might sound a little strange, but I was much better off after I figured it out. If you are like me and like to shower just before bed, following this routine will make you much more comfortable. The shower relaxes me and I sleep much more soundly if I do not stick to the sheets. The problem is that the temperature at bedtime is quite cold. My first attempt at taking a late-night shower left my teeth chattering and my toes all but frozen to the floor. I tried showering when I got back from the evening hunt, but that presented me with two problems. The first was taking a shower when I first returned to camp cut into the time allotted for sundowners, and I found this most unacceptable. Secondly, I still smelled like smoke when I climbed into bed. I had to figure out how to take a shower at bedtime that would not cause me to lose any body parts to frostbite. This method will work equally well if you are in a tent or a chalet. The only requirement is there has to be an adequate supply of hot water.

Here is how I do it. First, you finish all other bedtime preparations. This includes brushing your teeth, removing contact lenses, anything that would prevent you from getting into bed when you finish your shower. Then, you lay out your towel, polar fleece sweater, pajama bottoms, and bedroom slippers. Turn only the hot water on and let it run long enough to warm the shower floor and walls. This should be about as long as it takes you to get undressed, about a minute or minute and a half. Next, adjust the water temperature, step inside and shower as normal. When you are done and the water is off, do not exit the shower. Reach out, grab your towel, and dry only your face and torso. Wrap the towel around your waist, and put on the polar fleece sweater. Now you can exit the shower, dry your lower half, and put on your pajama bottoms and bedroom slippers. Your body will have enough heat left from the shower to give you time to towel dry and comb your hair. Head straight to bed and snuggle down under the covers. The heat your body stored from the shower and that you prevented from leaving with the polar fleece and pajama bottoms will transfer to the bed and, in no time, you will be snug and warm. If you cannot sleep with the polar fleece on (and I can't), wait until lights out to take it off. If you like to sleep with a shirt on, try a silk thermal top like the one I suggest on the "what to take list". Another good idea is to put your base layers for the next morning in the bed with you, they will be warm in the morning and allow you to dress without getting too much of a chill.

The last thing I want to cover in this chapter is also **hint number thirty-three: keep a daily journal.** This is so important that I can't stress it enough. You are paying a considerable sum to be in Africa hunting. If your mind is anything like mine, the little details of your trip will fade very quickly when you return to civilization and your normal life. Sure, you will remember the kudu bull that you took, but you will forget the family of warthogs that you almost spooked and thereby almost ruined the stalk before it even got started. You might remember sitting around the fire at night looking at the sky, but forget how bright the stars look with no ambient light to dull them. If you do not write the little things down, they will be lost forever. Take a few minutes each night after you are snuggled in bed to write in your journal. Do not wait even one day; if you do, you may forget something. It does not matter what you write in, because after you read it just one time when you get home, you will want to redo it. The memories will come back so clear that you will want to preserve them even better than you already have. It does not matter whether you type them and print them out or copy them by hand into a leather-bound keepsake, you will happy that you have them.

Journal on desk

CHAPTER EIGHT
The Hunt

Your hunting day will start early. Since we are going to be getting ourselves up, my definition of early might not be the same as yours. Breakfast will be between 5:30 am and 7:00 am, depending on the day's activities. I recommend being ready to walk to the truck as soon as breakfast is over. This means having everything that you want to take with you in your daypack and having your gun cased and ammo in your pocket. I would also suggest applying sunscreen before leaving camp using the mirror in the bath. It really helps keep missed spots from burning. **Hint number thirty-four: take all of your gear to breakfast with you so that you can leave as soon as breakfast is over.** The reason to take it to breakfast with you is, in the event that you have to answer the call of nature, all of your gear can be loaded for you and keep you from losing any hunting time. If all of your gear was in one spot, you can verify that nothing was left behind by simply looking at the spot on your way to the truck.

How much clothing to wear is something that you will also have to figure out first thing in the morning. It will probably take you a day or two to figure it out, but pay attention to how quickly things warm up during the day. I am not a cold-natured person by any means, but I normally start the day with just about all of the layers I have. Johann's truck is open and I love it that way but it is downright cold when it is thirty-some degrees and you have a 45 mph wind. The combination of the wind and cold make me really appreciate all of those layers. When you leave the truck, it becomes decision time. Do I keep all of the layers because it is still cold? Or do I leave them behind so that I do not have to keep up with them when it warms up? You have to decide that one for yourself. I tend to err on the side of being too cool. Therefore, when I leave the truck to start a stalk or hike, I peel my coat and sweater off and leave them with the truck. If I get hot and sweaty, I tire more easily than if I am slightly on the cool side. It will warm up soon and I normally generate enough body heat through physical exertion to stay warm until then anyway. To me, it is much easier to leave several layers in the truck than to tote them with you if you get too hot. Notice that I said leave the layers in the truck not just in the morning, but all day. If you take them out at lunch and leave them at camp, you will be most unhappy on the cold ride back.

What does a typical hunting day entail? The answer depends greatly on where you are and what you are hunting. I could be a good politician with that answer, could I not? All kidding aside, the answer boils down to three types of hunting. These three will not cover every circumstance, but they will cover better than ninety percent. The first type and the one most familiar to most Americans would be to sit in a concealed location and wait for the game to come to you, like hunting whitetail deer. In Africa, more often than not, this happens at a waterhole. Most animals have to drink daily, so the source of water is a natural place to wait. Unlike using an elevated stand here in the States, most blinds or hides in Africa are at ground level. This is good for hunters who cannot climb ladders or do not like heights, but it is worse, much worse, if you can't sit still and here is why. There are a lot more predatory animals in Africa than there are here in North America. That makes most every prey animal very nervous. Their senses are alert to any movement, noise or smell that is out of the ordinary. Me, I am worse than a five year old when it comes to being still. Both of my PHs have threatened me on more than one occasion with severe bodily harm if I did not quit fidgeting and be still. I guess that is the reason I love Africa so much is that sitting still for extended periods is not a major part of most of the hunting and I very rarely have to do it. The exception to that is hunting lion or leopard over bait. I have done it once, and it is the only still hunting that I will ask to do again. The hides are constructed well enough that a limited amount of movement is not too bad, but noise is strictly forbidden. The reason I will do this again is that I have become addicted to dangerous game hunting. There is something primal about two predators facing off against each other in the fading daylight. Either might be victorious over the other, but I sure hope it is I, rather than whatever is on the bait. The adrenalin rush that you feel when a leopard or lion is on the bait is worse than any "buck fever" you ever felt before. What is in your sights would not mind having you for the main course when it is finished with the bait. If there was ever a time to shoot straight it is now. You do not want one of these top predators mad at you and hungry at the same time. Fortunately, hunting cats over bait is not really on many first timers to-do list, but it is a type of still hunting.

Spot and stalk is the second type and most hunting in Africa is done in this manner. I dearly love it and I'll tell you why. One aspect of hunting that is extremely important to me is camaraderie. I enjoy team hunting. The team is made up of you, your PH and your tracker. Sometimes there may be another hunter or observer, more than one tracker, perhaps even a park ranger or game scout, but, most of the time, it is just the three of you. Each member of the team has his own job, but each member is fine with helping any other member out. Each has the other's back, and all are working together to complete the task at hand, which is getting you your trophy. I also enjoy stalking because I do not have to be quiet one hundred percent of the time. I do not advocate being a blabbermouth, but talking in low voices is ok unless you have your quarry in sight. The ability to carry on a conversation is part of my **hint number thirty-five: use the time spent walking in between stalks to learn from your PH or tracker.** Watch what they are doing and ask them to explain it. If you see a species of animal or plant you can't identify, ask them. The more you know about what is going on all around you, the more you will enjoy your hunt.

How do you find the animals to stalk? There are several ways. The first, and my favorite way to spot animals, is to ease along in the hunting truck and just look for animals. I like it because I can put 100% of my effort into seeing what is around me. I do not have to worry about being a klutz and stepping in a hole or on a snake. I find that not having to worry about where I am going allows me to better enjoy and appreciate what I am seeing as well. It doesn't matter whether you spot them in the distance or cut their tracks where they crossed the road, because the end result is the same. You have to access what you have seen and determine if it is worth taking the time to get a closer look. When you have made your assessment, you can choose to give chase or say, "let's look for something bigger" and drive on. If you have seen the animal and can glass it, the decision can be easy. Just look it over and say yes or no. Even though it is an unknown, don't be afraid to follow a track. It is uncanny how much information your PH and tracker can glean just from looking at a track. The surprise at the end of the stalk may be worth the effort. If you decide to go for it, then it is "game on" until you take the animal or abandon the stalk.

If the terrain does not allow just driving around, your best option is to travel between elevated locations and glass for animals. I have mixed emotions about this method. I love the view from an elevated observation post, but, for some reason, I am unable to spot game unless it is the last two days of the safari. It never fails that it takes me to the end of the safari to get my "eyes" back. When I say "eyes", I mean the ability to spot shapes and then translate the shapes into animals, or to be able to recognize which shadows to look in, or how to tell if that lump is just a lump or a game animal laying down. Since I do not spot the game that well, I am prone to just enjoying the scenery and having a short rest. When a likely looking animal is spotted, a war council is quickly convened to discuss strategy. Do we walk from here or take the truck a little closer? Are there other animals in between us and the animal we want to stalk? Can we get around them without spooking them? Which way is the wind blowing; can we get down wind without being spotted? Once a plan is determined, the stalk is on. This scene can and probably will be repeated many times during the day.

The last type of hunting is what I call the half-day march. To employ the half-day march, you must be reasonably sure your quarry is in the area. For instance, what if you cut the tracks of a herd of buffalo where they crossed a road? The herd had entered an area that is very thick and with limited road access. If you drive in the area, you might come upon the herd unexpectedly and spook them with the truck. There-fore, you park the truck and hoof it in yourself. This type of hunt, like everything else in life, has its good points and bad points.

The good point is the walk. You never feel quite so alive as when you are walking through the bush, not knowing what you may find, or what may find you. There is no safety net provided by the truck. There is nothing between you and Africa, but your PH and what you have learned. You also see more wildlife when you are walking. The noise from the truck can and does scare off animals and drown out sounds. These sounds can draw your attention to whatever made it and give you a better chance of seeing it. The very fact that you are walking quietly allows you to get up close to other animals. When Phil and I were hunting impala in Zimbabwe, we came upon an old bull elephant. We were able to walk to within thirty or forty yards without disturbing him. We watched for a few moments and then left as quietly as we had come. He never suspected we were there. The bad point is also the walk. If the game does not cooperate, you could literally end up walking for miles and the only thing you end up with is tired feet.

Whichever method you choose for your morning hunt, lunch is always a welcome break. Besides allowing for some much needed rest and food, it gives you and your PH a chance to compare notes and come up with an afternoon game plan. Bounce any ideas you have off him; you may have an idea or method that is not commonly employed in Africa. You and he may be able to combine two strategies into a completely new hunting method. Either way, the two of you will be getting to know each other better. After your nap is over and the heat of the day has passed, it is back into the truck for your afternoon hunt.

If you are successful, you may be back early enough to use my exception to the sit-and-wait method of hunting. If you are still in hunting mode after your earlier success and want to try something different, or you just want to enjoy some peace and quiet, go sit at a water hole to end the day. Sitting around a waterhole during the last thirty to forty-five minutes can be a really neat experience, and even I can sit still for that amount of time.

One evening, after a lot of walking, we finally headed back to the truck. The idea came up to take a short detour and stop at a waterhole. We stopped and sat down on a log that was up against some brush. It was a perfect situation, only about sixty yards away from the waterhole. Only a few minutes went by before the entertainment started. The birds were the first to show up. There were mostly doves, but a few sand grouse worked their way in as well. I was thoroughly amazed at the sheer number of the birds. After watching the birds we were treated to an acrobatic performance by two young jackals. The amount of energy spent playing was incredible. They bounced, pounced, ran, and turned somersaults and back flips. It was completely enthralling. After watching the jackals for a while, I returned my attention to the great flights of birds swarming in for an evening drink. I sat there for a few moments lamenting the fact that I did not have my shotgun. I could easily have taken enough for a few appetizers, or "starters" as they are called in camp. It then dawned on me that the blast from a shotgun would have ruined the tranquility of the evening and all of the wildlife would have disappeared. Instead of looking at a waterhole teeming with activity and life, I would have been looking at a lonely shallow mud hole. Sometimes it is difficult for hunters to enjoy just watching wildlife. We become goal oriented and become so focused on our task that we cannot see the wildlife for the animals. That quiet evening by the waterhole, I remembered how to appreciate the outdoors without taking anything back but memories.

If you have completed your game package early or just want to have some fun on a laid-back afternoon consider this next suggestion. **Hint number thirty-six: hunt guinea fowl with a .22.** Remember my story back in chapter one? If there is a .22 anywhere close to camp and you can borrow or rent it, do so. That afternoon, I had more lighthearted fun that I have had in a long time. I was hunting in Africa, taking game, under no pressure, laughing, and feeling like a twelve-year-old kid. If you are in your twenties that might not seem like such a big thing, but for a forty-six year old that is a big deal. If you have the chance to do this, remember the TV commercial and "just do it". I will make you a promise that you will have a fun afternoon.

To my knowledge, Africa has more huntable game species than anywhere else does in the world. Most often, the animals are broken up into two groups, plains game and dangerous game. Since I am an avid bird hunter, I will add a third group, avian. Plains game, which mostly consists of different types of antelope, and if you add in giraffes, hyenas, warthogs, baboons, and a few types of cats, that about covers it. These animals live in varied terrains, anything from mountains, to savannah, to bushveld. Even though not all animals live in all locations, they are for the most part widely distributed.

The next group is dangerous game. This group consists of seven animals. They are the elephant, lion, leopard, Cape buffalo, rhinoceros, hippopotamus, and crocodile. Though other animals can and sometimes do kill people, this group is most often to blame. Dangerous game is not as widespread as it once was. These animals are only allowed to live where man thinks they should live. Thankfully, there are still many places in Africa where man is in the minority, and it is in these places that you will find dangerous game.

Why I would include a third group greatly puzzles some, but I would feel negligent if I left them out. Though not as widespread as some of the other game species, Africa has more birds than you think. There are: francolin, doves, sand grouse, guinea fowl, pigeons, and waterfowl. Best of all, the populations are healthy and the shooting can be fast and furious. That is one of the things that I like best about bird hunting. Instead of one good shot and you're done, you have the opportunity for many good shots. Spending an afternoon using up a box of shells and taking a good number of game birds not only puts food on the table, it is one of my favorite ways to spend time in the outdoors.

There are three major differences between North American game and African game. The first is size. African plains game varies greatly in size, but quite a few will weigh between five hundred and eight hundred pounds, and are very thick skinned. A huge whitetail, where I come from, is around one hundred and eighty pounds and thin skinned. The vital organs of African plains game are also in a slightly different location; they are farther forward. What does all of this add up to? It translates to the importance of shot placement. While shot placement is important in any type of hunting, you need to pay extra attention to it while hunting African game. I am not going to try to tell you where to shoot for every species of African animal. Other writers have done much better than I ever could. What I am going to do is give you another hint.

Hint number thirty-seven: the next time a gift giving reason rolls around, ask your spouse for a book. In addition to getting a good laugh at the look of disbelief on their face, it might help them to gain a little interest in your dream of going on a safari. There are a few good books out there, but I am partial to "The Perfect Shot", by Kevin Robertson. Kevin Robertson is a veterinarian as well as a PH. If anyone can tell you where to hit an animal to put it down quickly, he can. The book provides pictures of the animal with the best places to shoot shown on the picture. Next, he puts an overlay of the skeleton and internal organs on the same picture. When you look at the picture collectively you are able to see what the bullet will hit if you put it where you are supposed to. The book also gives you information on trophy selection, scoring, hunting methods, and rifle caliber suggestions. The book does have one very serious drawback. It does such a good job of describing the animals, it will probably entice you take multiple trips to complete your trophy wish list. My personal wish list is so long that every time my wife sees it or I mention it, I get the evil eye for at least thirty minutes. Whether you get this book or one of the others available, keep it close by and study it every chance you get. Doing so will ensure that you know where to shoot and keep your safari fresh in your mind.

My next rule is one that is important enough that it gets its own section. It is one that I live by, and I think all hunters should adopt at least some version of it. **Hint number thirty-eight: even though your PH can tell you when, or if to shoot, only you can decide if the shot is for you**. Let me explain what I mean by this. On day two of my first Cape buffalo hunt, I was on the shooting sticks with a good-looking bull in front of me. Phil had given me the ok to shoot. When I did not pull the trigger, he started urging me more strongly to take the shot. That progressed to him saying "shoot!" in a voice loud enough that the buffalo heard it. What Phil did not know was that when the shooting sticks were set up, they were located so that a single leaf from a bush blocked my view every time I got my eye to the scope. I could sort of see the buffalo but not nearly clear enough for me to take what I considered ethical shot. Only you know your abilities and if you can make the shot with what you are presented with. Do not get caught up in the heat of the moment and take a bad shot or one that is beyond your capabilities. It is easy to do and all of us will probably take one of these bad shots some time in our hunting careers. If you are lucky, you will either have a clean kill or a clean miss. The probable result is a wounded animal and, in Africa, a wounded animal can kill you. Do not wait until you are on the shooting sticks to start thinking about the shot. If you are too far away or at an uncomfortable angle, tell your PH and move. If you blow the stalk, you blow the stalk. I guarantee that your PH will prefer a blown stalk to a wounded and lost animal.

Getting in shape is every hunter's least favorite thing to do before going on a hunt. I am no exception to this myself. I would put off getting in shape until just before the hunt, and then pretend that I was eighteen again and almost kill myself by doing six months of exercise in six weeks. Then, something happened that changed my mind about getting in shape just before a hunt forever. I actually got in shape well before a hunt and had one of the most enjoyable hunts ever. There was no stopping to take a breather, "no you go on, and I'll catch up". I was even able to climb kopjes at a slow but steady pace. Walking all day, while tiring, was not exhausting, and I had energy left at the end of the day to really enjoy myself in camp. I lifted weights, and did enough cardio every weekday morning that I felt good. **Hint number thirty-nine: establish an exercise routine, and stick with it.**

I put a small TV in my basement where my exercise equipment is. It allowed me to exercise for thirty minutes every morning while I was doing something I did anyway. I used to set my alarm for thirty minutes before I had to get up so that I could lie in bed and watch the morning news. I decided to get up just five minutes earlier and watch the news while I exercised. What a difference just five minutes a day made. That's right, I changed my wake-up time by five minutes and used the time better. I have to admit that I am still a little wider than I was in my twenties, but most of us are by the time we get to be fifty. I can, however, walk all day long, climb, and even run short distances without falling out. If I do wind myself, I can usually get my breathing under control enough to make a shot in less than sixty seconds. I hit upon this earlier, but you should add something to your workout to simulate exertion under hunting circumstances. This would be running in a crouched position while carrying a load to simulate a rifle, and tip toeing at a fast pace. Both of these absolutely killed me on my last hunt, and I decided that wouldn't ever happen again. I do not incorporate these in to my daily routine, but I will add them about two months before my next hunt.

Let's pretend that you have put everything that you have learned together and you have just taken your first African game animal. Now what do you do? Snap a few pictures and head off to the skinning shed? I think not. You have spent considerable time and money to get to this point. Are a few hastily taken snapshots going to be enough? **Hint number forty is to plan out your trophy photo shoot. I would suggest writing the plan down and then going over it with your PH.** Writing it down and keeping it in your pocket may sound a little overboard, but it is not. Consider what is going on at this particular moment. You have just taken an African trophy, and your heart rate and adrenalin level will be elevated. There is this blur of activity going on around you, and your PH and tracker are busy removing grass and rocks that will be in the picture. They are posing your trophy the same way they have posed hundreds of trophies before. All of this is being done while they are congratulating you, shaking hands, and slapping backs. Before you know it, the trophy is in the truck and you are back to camp. In all fairness to the PHs out there, they really do want you to have a good picture, but they just get on auto pilot sometimes. This is simply because they have done it so many times before and are comfortable with the procedure. Here are some of the things that you should consider: lighting, position, background, and camera angle. While everyone else is busy preparing for the pictures, take a minute and look around you and make a few mental notes.

Where is the sun? Is it overhead, behind you or in front of you? Where do you want it to be in reference to the picture? Normally you would want the sun to be in front of you, but if it is early or late in the day and you are squinting, that makes a bad picture. I know this from experience. When I took my kudu, it was late in the day and the sun was almost set.

How not to take a picture

I was behind the kudu holding its horns the way Johann showed me. The sun was very bright and I was squinting so furiously that I looked like I was holding up four or five hundred pounds and was going to drop it at any second. The picture would have been much better if we had rotated the kudu about forty-five degrees and I had not been looking into the sun. Are there any shadows that would conceal anything in the picture? Since a lot of African animals' camouflage uses shading and shadowing, an errant shadow could cause problems. If it is twilight, try playing with the flash. Use it to fill in shadowy spots or to add definition. Another option is to try a slow shutter speed to capture the most realistic image possible.

Much Better

Hint number forty-one is to wash the blood off your trophy before any pictures are taken. While the blood might not bother you, it might bother some of your non-hunting friends. While the animal is being rinsed off, decide what position do you want the trophy to be in and where you will be in relation to the trophy. The standard animal on its stomach and you behind the animal can be boring. Take one of these if you like, but don't stop there. Try laying the animal on its side with the head and neck turned so that the head is resting on its chin, facing away from its rear end. If you get on one knee to the rear of the animal and the picture is taken from the ground level, you can get some really neat pictures. For smaller animals, lay it across your shoulders and behind your neck, and pretend to carry it out. Just remember that you will probably get bloody. If there is anything interesting in the background, use it. If the sun is setting or rising, or there is an interesting mountain, tree, rock, or river, add them into the mix. Be sure to remember to frame yourself and the trophy off to the side a little, so that the trophy and background do not compete with each other.

One of my favorite pictures is my cape buffalo stretched out with my rifle hanging on the shooting sticks in the background. No people, nothing but the grass, sky, buffalo, and my rifle hanging by its strap on the shooting sticks. Be sure to include your PH, tracker(s), game scout, or anyone else who helped with the hunt. This was a team effort, so get a team photo. Remember to smile and remind your PH to smile. Johann is one of the nicest, friendliest, most fun people to be around that I have ever met. That said, he was hell bent on looking serious and professional in every trophy picture I took my first time out with him. When I got back home, everyone asked me why I was hunting with a mercenary. I still like to kid him about this from time to time. If your PH wants a serious picture, let him have one, but get him to smile in one as well. This is a time for celebration; you have accomplished a goal that you have set for yourself. Be sure to reflect that in some of the pictures.

Be sure to vary the camera position to get different effects. Generally, if the picture is taken with the camera almost at ground level, the animal will look bigger. Take multiple pictures with multiple camera locations and see what looks the most realistic to you. Try some pictures that are not ninety degrees from the trophy. Different distances will change the effect of the photo as well. Take some that are up close, what I call a head-and-shoulders shot. Simply stated, it is just the head and shoulders of the animal with your head and shoulders behind it. Then back up and take a few pictures where you and the whole trophy fill the frame. If time allows, take pictures from several distances. This will change the scale of you and your trophy and give you a different look.

Hint number forty-two is to bring a small tripod for group or timed exposure shots. I like a little gadget called a "gorilla pod". It is a small tripod with flexible legs that you can wrap tightly around a tree limb, roll bar, fence post, or just about anything else to aid you in taking a picture. This gadget will come in handy for the team photo and for shots without a flash in low light.

After the hunt, it is time to load the animal in the truck. If it is an impala, it is no big deal. If it is a seven hundred pound kudu, that is a whole other matter. Depending on the size of your hunting party and the equipment available, you might want to help load. First off, it is just good manners to help out. Secondly, if the animal is dropped for lack of manpower and a horn snaps off, you have a problem. I told you already about having to cut my buffalo in half to get it in the truck, and that worked just fine, but it was labor intensive. Johann has a rig that makes loading simple and it reminds me of something that one of my first bosses taught me.

His name was Alan Moose. He told me something one time that I have always remembered and I have tried to live by it. I was struggling to get a 55-gallon drum of construction hardware out of the back of a pickup. He watched me struggle for a few minutes before he decided to impart his words of wisdom to me. To make them more memorable, he proved their usefulness with a demonstration. He got on a forklift, raised the blades above the height of the trucks sidewalls, and pulled up to the truck at a ninety-degree angle. Next, he took a piece of chain off the back lift, made one loop around the barrel, and one loop over one blade on the forklift. He raised the barrel up, easy as you please, and set it down where he wanted it. After he shut the lift off, he told me, "What your brain doesn't do, your back has to", and I have never forgotten it. What does that have to do with Johann's method of loading of heavy game? I will explain.

Johann had his land cruiser truck fitted with an electric winch, a push bar, a roll bar, and an elongated tailgate that would reach the ground when lowered. There was also a large pulley welded to front of the push bar and the top of the roll bar. Whenever he had to load a heavy animal, all he had to do was back up to it and drop the tailgate. Next, he pulled out the winch line, put it over the pulley on the push bar, then the pulley on the roll bar, and, finally, around the head of the animal. As soon as he hit the switch to activate the winch, the animal is pulled across the tailgate and into the bed of the truck. It was one of the coolest things I have ever seen. It epitomizes the mantra of what your brain doesn't do your back has to. I have never seen a rig like it anywhere else.

Note the long tailgate and pulleys on the push and roll bars

Sorry for being sidetracked, but I thought it was an interesting story and a good life lesson. Anyway, on the way back, decide if you want to go to camp or the skinning shed. More often than not you are taken back to camp so you can get cleaned up, but if you want to go by the skinning shed just ask. Watching the skinners work is like watching the chefs at the Kanki steak house. As soon as they raise the animal up off the floor, the knives start slapping against each other or sharpening steel in order to freshen up the razor sharp edge. When the skinners feel the knives are sharp enough, they move in a coordinated team effort to get the animal dressed out and skinned. If animal skinning were ever an Olympic team event, the guys from the African hunting camps would win hands-down. I do not go to the skinning shed on every hunt, but I do stop by every once in a while just to watch the spectacle. If you have not already talked with your PH about what kind of trophy mount you want, do so while the hanging and knife sharpening are going on. The type of mount you want will make a huge difference in how your animal is prepared for the taxidermist.

CHAPTER NINE

Taxidermy and Getting Your Trophy Home

The first thing that you need to know about taxidermy is what kind of mount you want. That should be a simple enough decision. For me, it became a little more complicated after a visit to an African taxidermy shop. Most of us are familiar with a head mount or a shoulder mount, where the neck and head or part of the shoulders plus the neck and head are preserved. A few of us have seen a full-body mount or a skin turned into a rug. Until I visited the shop for the first time, I had never heard of a European mount or a pedestal mount, or seen furniture, lamps, or pillows made from animal products. Suddenly, there were a lot more options that I had to consider. Let me try to give you a brief description of the other options.

A European mount is just the bleached skull and horns by themselves or on a finished shield. It can be quiet striking with the bright white skull on a dark shield. Just in case they are called something else in other areas, a "shield" is a finished piece of wood, normally in the shape of a shield that the attaches to the back of the trophy. My personal preference is to preserve the animal as it was when it was alive, but you should be aware that the European mount is available and it is considerably less expensive. The pedestal mount is made to sit on a table or the floor and is well, a pedestal. This mount is could be used for something tall like a giraffe or any mount that you do not want to display on the wall. The option of furniture and pillows made from parts of the animal is another area that does not really interest me, but tanning and keeping the hides for a project is another matter. I have seen some really nice gun cases made from the hides of wild game and have decided to have one made from my last trophies. **Hint number forty-three is to visit a local taxidermist before you leave Africa.** This hint may not be practical if you fly into a remote camp but, if you can visit a taxidermist, it is a good idea. It is a must, if you plan to have your taxidermy work done in Africa.

On my first trip to Africa, I had taken three of the four trophies in my package fairly quickly, and Johann asked me if I wanted to take a morning off and go into town and visit the local taxidermist. Not really realizing why at the time, I agreed. We left right after breakfast the next morning. It was a pleasant drive in, and I was able to meet his gunsmith when we stopped by to leave a rifle to have a silencer put on it. When I asked about the silencer, he mumbled something about "those blankety-blank baboons" and damage to equipment. We spent the rest of the trip talking about how a country that was serious about the number and types of guns they let into the country had no problems with silencers. Lest I get too far off track, the rest of that story will have to wait until another time. The first taxidermist we came to was a huge operation. There must have been sixty or more people working there. Everyone seemed to be busy. We let ourselves in to the show room and looked around. The work was good and the animals looked real. We finally got a price list and talked to a salesperson for a few minutes before excusing ourselves and leaving. The second shop we visited was much smaller. Sylvia met us at the front door and showed us into the show room. When I looked closely at the animals, I could see a difference. These not only looked real; they looked like they were still alive. She even took us out back into the work areas of the shop so I could see what went on behind the scenes. After visiting for a short time, I had just about made up my mind to let Sylvia do the work. A quick check of her pricing confirmed it.

Why would you choose to get the taxidermy done in Africa as opposed to in the United States? There are several reasons for and several against; I'll try to give you an honest look at both sides. Cost might seem like an issue, but it really is not. This is how the pricing has worked out for me so far. It is cheaper to have the work done in Africa, but it is more expensive to have the finished trophies shipped to the United States. It is less expensive to ship the hide and skull to the U.S., but labor is more expensive here. The only two times I priced it both ways, it was less than one hundred dollars' difference.

If cost is not a factor, what is? I think the fact that the African taxidermist sees and deals with the animals on a daily basis is a factor. To me, someone who sees an animal a lot can make a more lifelike trophy than someone who only sees the animal occasionally, if at all. If your local taxidermist has experience with African animals, that is a different story. If he has done good work for you in the past, there is a reasonable expectation that he will do good work in the future. There is no one within reasonable driving distance of me that has experience with more than just one or two African animals. I could have gone on the Web or looked in the back of my hunting and fishing magazines, but I really like meeting a person face to face if I am going to be giving them my hard-earned money. Time is another consideration, one that either method can really claim an advantage over the other. So far, my in-Africa taxidermy projects have been delivered to me in just about a year. The raw materials

I had shipped to the U.S. arrived in nine months, and the local work should take three to four months or about a year. What would be the drawbacks of using an African taxidermist? The biggest one is you have no recourse if the trophy comes to you completely botched. It is too expensive to ship it back. In addition, to have it redone here, if you find a local taxidermist to try to fix it, it would be expensive. If I have thoroughly confused you and you don't what to do and where to do, it let me try to clear up the confusion.

Remember way back in the beginning at hint number three — to listen to your PH as if your life depended on it, because it very well could? If you can trust him with your life, proceed to **hint number forty-four: ask him to take you to the taxidermist he personally uses and, if possible, and if it is feasible, would he please check on your trophy when it is ready to ship**. If he will do this, you have an ace in the hole. When the taxidermist notifies you that your trophy is finished, have him notify your PH as well. If the taxidermist knows your PH will be coming by to inspect your trophies before they leave his shop, he will double check everything before your PH gets there, preventing the problem in the first place. If there is a problem, your PH will make sure that the trophy meets his standards before it leaves. He will, in essence, be your advocate at the taxidermy shop.

I have been more than pleased with the work at Otjwarongo Taxidermy. Sylvia is one of those unique individuals that can remember a name of someone that she met over a year ago and she always makes me feel welcome. I have never had a reason to be dissatisfied with any of the work that her shop has done for me. If you hunt in the central to northern part of Namibia, stop by and check out her shop. They do good work. They do such good work that I wanted them to do my buffalo and impala from last summer's Zimbabwe hunt. Unfortunately, I was unable to get the proper permits to be able to send the trophies to Namibia. I was also in a remote fly-in camp and therefore unable to visit a taxidermist in Zimbabwe. I was in a quandary as to what to do. I finally decided to venture into uncharted waters, at least as far as I was concerned. My local taxidermist is very good and has done work for me for years. He has hunted Africa and done his own trophies, but that is about it. He has agreed to do the work for me. The hides are still at the tannery, so this is a work in progress. I'll have to let you know how it works out.

Shipping your trophy back home is expensive, and I do not know of a way around it. The main reason is that most of the trophies that come into the U.S. come by air. Two of my more recent shipments of trophies one in 2007 and the other in 2008 were both about $1,800.00. This included the packing, crating, and insurance. The raw materials from my August 2009 hunt in Zimbabwe arrived in April 2010 and the cost was about $1,200.00. Just for the record, the Taxidermy work is going to run about $500.00 more than, if Sylvia had done it. I have had experience with two different shipping companies and have had no problems with either company.

There is one last piece of the shipping puzzle and cost that we need to go over and that is clearing U.S. Customs and the U.S. Fish and Wildlife Service. Unless you just happen to live near one of the eighteen USFWS-designated airports, have extra time, and the patience to deal with paperwork, I suggest that you employ a Customs Broker or Expediter. This person or company deals with all of the above on a daily basis. They can handle the paperwork, and will know the ins and outs of dealing with government agencies. They will also take care of getting your trophies to a freight company for their final delivery to you. If you would like to employ one of these companies, your Booking Agent will probably be able to recommend one to you. I have used only one, Fauna and Flora in

New York, and Matt has always taken good care of me. The charges are in the six-to-seven-hundred-dollar range. That includes all paperwork, dealing with US Customs, USFWS and freight from New York to North Carolina. This might sound expensive, but, if you compare it with my other option, it really is not. My closest USFWS-designated airport is five and a half hours and three hundred twenty miles away. If I did it myself, it would take one day each way to drive and two days there to do paperwork and wait for it to clear. If I added up the cost of three nights in a hotel, four days' worth of food, gasoline, and other miscellaneous expenses, it would probably be very close to the cost of having it done. If I included the cost for the four days' worth of my time, the cost would exceed what the customs broker would charge. A possible exception might be if you had family or friends in the area that you could stay with that would help defray some of the cost. Staying with family or friends would also alleviate some of the boredom factor and, therefore, make doing it yourself a possibility. The decision is up to you.

This is sort of a minor thing but it can be helpful. Even if you think you are probably going to have the work done in Africa, take some shipping labels for your local taxidermist with you. Be sure to include some for your home address and some for your customs broker, as well. At the end of your hunt, have your PH or Safari operator attach the labels to your trophy(s). This will accomplish two things. The first is that it will label your trophies as yours and help avoid a possible mix up later. Secondly, it will avoid any mix up, or "lost in translation", in getting the trophies to where you need them to go.

All totaled, getting two to four trophies from the bush to your living room is going to cost you about $4,500.00 in 2010 dollars. The good news is that, in the last four years, the prices have remained constant. I personally think they will stay in this range until the global economy settles down. The only exception to this would be if something severely disrupted the oil supply and jet fuel went way up. I wanted to include this information because I could not find it anywhere and was a little shocked at the cost it added to my first safari. I want to save you from this unpleasant surprise at the end of your first safari. The experience of your first safari should hold nothing but pleasant memories for you. Knowing the total cost upfront with no gotch-ya's at the end of your trip should allow just that.

CHAPTER TEN
Be a Considerate Guest

I am going to assume that I am preaching to the choir here, but I want to mention several things that I consider important enough to bring to everyone's attention. Americans sometimes get a reputation of being rude and self-centered. I think most of this is unintentional and comes from our lifestyle. It is so different from most everywhere else on the planet. In my opinion, Americans, as a rule, are so goal–oriented, and in such a hurry to accomplish said goal, that we fail to see the effects our actions have on the other people around us. When we fail to notice how our actions affect others around us, we can be perceived as uncaring or just plain rude. I am no exception to this myself. I constantly have to remind myself when I travel abroad that the world does not revolve around what I want. There is a saying that I learned on a sailing cruse to the Caribbean, and that saying is **hint number forty-five: set your internal clock to "Island Time".** When we came aboard, the mate asked us to leave our worries and hectic lifestyles behind because we were now on "island time". Island time can be best described as a state of being that happens somewhere between a half to three quarters speed of real time. There are no worries. Everything that needs to happen will happen, maybe not as soon as I think it should, but it will happen. I try to adopt this frame of mind as soon as I step out of my front door on the way to every vacation. If I can do this, little delays and bumps in the road do not bother me near as badly. As a direct result of that, I am more relaxed, and therefore nicer to everyone around me. It works so well that sometimes my wife will look at me and say "island time" to remind me to relax and slow down. In the years since I discovered my passion for safaris, I have modified this to also apply to Africa. It is now "African time" while I am on safari. I am not saying to let people to walk all over you. If you have a complaint or problem, let someone know, just do it in a calm and polite manner, you will be much happier with the results. After all, if your host does not know there is a problem, how can they fix the problem?

The next item from my soapbox is being a considerate guest. This includes many different aspects. Keeping your quarters neat is one. The house keeping staff is there to clean your room and take care of you during your stay, but do not abuse the service. Put your gear where it goes; don't leave items strewn about everywhere. Put your dirty clothes in the hamper and not on the floor, you remember, just like your mom taught you. Being considerate also means: do not drink too much alcohol. Since I have already said how much I enjoy sundowners, you might think that I may be prone to partake of one too many. While I do enjoy several, I am constantly watching my time piece to keep me from drinking too many cocktails or glasses of wine with dinner in too short a time frame. I have a self-imposed cut off that kicks in if I have a drink before I check my watch so see how much time has lapsed since my last drink. Having too much of a buzz can cause you big problems in Africa. The following story should give you an idea of how.

We were sitting around the fire one night after dinner and having a good time. I had my usual glass of after-dinner something or other and was enjoying the conversation and winding down my evening. Out of the darkness, about forty or fifty yards beyond the boma enclosing our fire, we heard a long, low whining noise followed by a muffled "rrrrrrrrrrrr". The conversation stopped while we waited for it to repeat. This time we heard it more clearly and Johann identified the sound as a leopard killing a kudu calf. He dashed into the tent, grabbing his rifle and spotlight. He told me to follow him as he went past me toward the noise. Now I was not sure I wanted to be outside with that noise in any way shape or fashion, but it took me only a second to know that in order for this to precede safely, Johann needed back up. I was more than a little relieved when he got in the hunting truck, instead of taking off on foot. We took off through the bush just outside of camp to where we thought the noise came from. Even though the headlights from the truck and the spotlight lit up the bushveld, we never did find our quarry. My point in all of this is that, if I had been incapacitated from too much drink, I would have put Johann and myself at risk. Being drunk in camp is not good for anyone.

Next on my list of being considerate is to be on time in the morning. Your camp staff and PH have been up and preparing the camp for your day. Being late makes breakfast cold and soggy and forces your PH and tracker to work harder in able to start your hunt on time. If you are tired and want to take a morning off to catch a few extra winks, that is not a problem; just let everyone know ahead of time.

The next two items are sort of related and I'll cover them at the same time. Think before you speak and do not be a know it all. All PHs appreciate having an experienced hunter in camp. The experience often makes their jobs easier and more fun. Where experience causes problems is if the client thinks he knows more than the PH does. It makes for a long day for the PH if his client is constantly complaining that somebody else did something this way, or it would work better if we did it like I did it with so and so. I have never met a PH that was not open to suggestions or questions about why something is done in a certain way. They love to share their knowledge, but they do not need to have to justify their actions. If you need more explanation or do not understand, just politely ask for clarification. Just think a little bit about what you want to say or ask before you open your mouth to speak. If you are unsure how something will go over, just ask yourself if you would like it if someone did it to you.

Practice ethical hunting at all times and do not put your PH in the position of fudging a regulation to comply with your request. This one is easy. Just practice what you have learned when you were a youngster — know your maximum shot range, do not shoot through brush, and be sure of what is behind your target — and all of the other rules given to you by whoever taught you how to hunt. I also want to repeat something I said earlier: only you can decide whether to shoot or not. If you are uncomfortable with the shot in any way, do not pull the trigger. It is better to back off and start over, even if it means blowing the stalk, than to wound and lose an animal, especially a dangerous animal.

My last suggestion in being considerate is also my last hint. **Hint number forty-six: consider yourself a guest in someone's home**. If you act like a guest, you should never go wrong. Since you are considering yourself a guest, think about taking a housewarming gift, nothing expensive or fancy but something that may be hard to find in Africa. Each location is different, but here is a list of a few suggestions. Plastic ammo boxes seem to be in short supply and quite expensive in some locations and they are always handy. I recommend the twenty-round size with the slip-on-and-off top. Use your early communications with your PH to determine what caliber he shoots so that you will know what size ammo box to get. Good, compact flashlights are also nice. If you can, choose one that uses regular batteries, as some of the specialty batteries are not available. If your PH reloads his own cartridges, empty brass is nice, and if he shoots the same caliber you decide to use, take him some premium ammunition. Just remember that the ammunition has to match a rifle that you take with you. Most countries only allow you to bring in ammunition that goes with your rifle. One last thought: if you are uncomfortable giving a gift up-front, give them at the end of the trip. I do not think it is very likely, but if, for some reason, you and your PH do not get along, you can simply leave the items in your suitcase and take them home. These are just a few suggestions to put you in the right track should you choose to get aboard. Like everything else, it is up to you.

The last thing I want to talk about is gratuities. I have asked a great many people over the years about leaving a tip at the end of the hunt. At best, I have gotten bits and pieces of answers, but never a complete and useful answer. I have talked with PHs, owners, booking agents, other hunters, and even asked around in safari hunting chat rooms. Not one ever gave me a straight-up answer. The answers ranged from ten percent of the daily rate to five percent of the total bill. I have heard ten percent of the daily rate for just the PH, unless he is also the owner, in which case he gets enough from the regular bill and therefore no tip. I have heard straight-up amounts from $500.00 to $1000.00, with another couple hundred added for the staff. I even had one camp give me a list of staff and the amount they expected for the staff, but no set amount for the PH. I have been told to give the tip to the PH for distribution to the other staff, and then to be sure to distribute the tips to the staff myself. As you might guess, I was left completely confused as to who gets a tip and how much that tip should be. When I finally put all of the pieces together, I decided I have been doing it wrong.

Now I am going to give you as straight answer as I can, even though I run the risk of making someone somewhere mad at me. This is also what

I am going to be doing on all future safaris. I based these figures on each individual doing their job to the best of their abilities and doing it with a smile. Hunting success does not enter in the equation. What matters is effort and attitude. If they have busted their backsides and the game has not cooperated, that is the nature of hunting. As far as the rest of the camp goes, if your quarters stay clean and neat, your food is well-prepared and flavorful, the cook and maid deserve a tip. Your tracker, who has been there with you every day in the field and probably walked more steps than you have, deserves a tip. If you have a government game scout that has pitched in to help and shared his knowledge, tip him also. The skinner that takes care to make sure the cape of your trophy is in good shape when it gets to the taxidermist should receive something also.

Here is what I suggest. For the PH, regardless if he is the owner or lowest man on the totem pole, should get between five and ten percent of the total daily rate. The reason for the variance is that daily rates vary so much between locations. If you are on a package, back the trophy fees out, and add a percent or two, then divide that number by the number of days in camp to get a daily-rate figure. Your tracker should get at least $100.00 delivered by you to him personally. The same goes for a game scout that pitches in and helps with the hunt. Housekeeping and the cook staff should get at least $50.00-$75.00. The rest of the staff, including the laundry, grounds keeping, and maintenance, should not be excluded either. After I give the PH, tracker, and game scout their tip, I will give the PH the rest of the tip, along with any specific amounts for distribution to the rest of the staff. If you have had personal interaction with, or had exceptional service given by another staff member and want to thank the personally, that is ok too. When all is said and done, I want the total of the tips to be between ten and fifteen percent of the daily rate total. I purposely left a range here to try to allow for everyone's comfort range. Personally, if I was on a twenty-one day safari with a $1000.00

daily rate, I would be uncomfortable leaving a $3000.00 plus tip, simply because I never made that kind of money and the amount seems, to my personal comfort level, excessive. On the other hand, if I am on a fourteen-day plains game safari with a daily rate of $250.00, a total tip of $625.00 seems a little low. These amounts are just suggestions and the tip is really up to you based on your perceived level of service and what you ultimately decide is fair.

Now it is time to plan your safari, get on "African time", and enjoy what will be one of the best times of your life. A story about one of my best times is coming up next. Happy hunting.

CHAPTER ELEVEN

Safari, Family Style

I was one of those poor, unfortunate saps that caught a fatal dose of "Safari fever" on my first trip to Africa. "Safari fever" so ingrained the safari lifestyle into me that hunting in Africa was all I wanted to talk about. The good news is there is a remedy for this particular fever. The bad news about this particular disease is you are unaware that you have it until someone who has been to Africa notices your symptoms and diagnoses your condition. There is no cure, but the disease can go into temporary remission by taking one simple treatment. That treatment is to return to Africa. As you step off the plane and take a deep breath, the symptoms will start to ease, just enough to allow you to get to camp. Complete remission only occurs as when you get to camp and scuff up a little of the fine African dust with your boots. Once I had been properly diagnosed, and informed of the cure, I spent almost every waking moment plotting and scheming how to get back to Africa. Much to my chagrin, my trying to send my condition into remission caused a lot of stress in my family life. This stress and familial upheaval led me to try an expensive, risky, and desperate decision. I decided to take my family to Africa. If they could just go there, maybe, just maybe, they would understand what I had been through and show me just a little compassion. I also stood a risk on them being infected with the same disease that had worked its way into my core. It was a risk that I had to take.

The other members of my family are all female. Janice is my wife of twenty-six years. We have two daughters, Kristine, who was nineteen at the time and Jessica who was fifteen. Planning a safari for girls, and one that would allow me time to hunt, was a daunting task, one I knew very little about. I, at least, knew where to start. My first call was to Rick. He immediately told me not to worry, that he had planned many safaris for a great many women and that he had not lost a husband yet. After we talked for a while, we ended the conversation with him promising to gather some information and get back to me. In the meantime, I was to inform the girls of my intentions and have them start thinking about what they wanted to do. I also fired off a few e-mails to Johann and Vera to let them know what I was up to and to get their input. I also needed them to check their calendar to see what dates were available. I knew that I was going to have to do some saving to afford this trip, so we picked a date that was twenty months out. It took some planning and a lot of e-mails and phone calls, but we came up with a plan that seemed to suit everyone.

I then proceeded to mess things up when I came up with a hair-brained idea that, if it worked well, would lead to an unbelievable trip for all. If it didn't, my name would be mud for at least a few decades. We would be in Africa just six weeks before my twenty-fifth wedding anniversary. That gave me the bright idea to have Janice and I repeat our vows with an African ceremony. I also wanted to do this as a surprise gift to my wife. I know that some of you are thinking that I am absolutely crazy, and I may have been. I was, after all, suffering from "safari fever" and probably was not in my right mind. Without getting ahead of myself let me tell you what happened.

Rick, true to his word, sent me a package of literature that he had picked up in Namibia that described a fair number of tourist attractions. Over the next few weeks, Janice and the girls looked them over, did research on the Internet, and formulated a list of what they wanted to do. In the meantime, I e-mailed Vera to tell her and Johann my idea to surprise Janice. Vera, God bless her, took the idea and ran with it. We started scheming and planning, without Janice or either of my daughters finding out anything. One of our biggest problems was how to get the girls to take a nice dress to Africa without telling them what was happening. Vera solved the problem with the idea to have a costume party. I was to tell the girls that, while we were visiting Africa, Johann's father was going to be having a birthday and there was going to be a surprise party for him. The genius part was the surprise party was also going to be a costume party. The theme was going to be the movie "Out of Africa", and the dress was going to be formal safari wear! It was a phenomenal idea and, from there, the rest of the rest of the plans came together. Over the next year, there were a lot of e-mails back and forth to work out the exact details. We even brought my daughters in on the plan when Janice said she could not find "formal Safari wear". With the girls in on things, they could gently push their mom in the right direction. I have already told you about the trip over, so I'll start after I cleared customs and met Johann.

When we left the airport, we headed southwest toward the world's oldest desert and the world's tallest sand dunes. The Namib Desert runs almost the entire length of the Namibian coastline. Janice really wanted to see the desert with its huge, red sand dunes. The dunes can be several hundred meters high and are quite a spectacular sight. To get to the desert, we had to go through a mountain range and that was a neat experience in itself. The drive was a leisurely but long one. The girls did not seem to mind as they got their first look at African animals — kudu, gemsbok, springbuck, and baboons made an appearance during the trip.

La Mirage

Kristine & Jessica in their room

We got to our lodging after dark and quickly checked in. "Le Mirage" was more than Johann had promised. To me it looked like a Moroccan castle. All the walls were stone, and there were even observation turrets. When you first entered, the resort there was an inner courtyard that looked like an oasis, complete with grass, palm trees, and water (in this case a swimming pool). It was a neat place for our first night in Africa. At dinner, the girls got their first taste of African cuisine. Dinner was five courses that consisted of some kind of egg appetizer, fish soup, a pasta salad, kudu steak, and a dessert made with pears and chocolate. After dinner, everyone was pretty tired and ready to turn in. We also had to be up well before daylight the next morning, as we had scheduled a hot air balloon ride to watch the sunrise over the dunes. I did not want to let the evening end, so I tried to get everyone to go stargazing, but it proved to be a futile effort. The girls all wanted to turn in and get some rest. I am man enough to know when I am licked, so I gave up and turned in as well. We got a disappointing phone call the next morning notifying us of the cancellation of our balloon tour. The winds were too strong and it was just not safe to go up. Johann and I regrouped, and we decided to pile everyone back in the car and drive to the Soussevlei to see the sunrise there.

The name Soussevlei loosely translates to "open place of nothingness". The attraction was sort of lost on me, but, as long as everyone else was happy, I was good with it. Janice got her pictures and a little extra. We had stopped at one of the observation points, and she and the girls went off to climb the dunes. Unbeknownst to them, Johan and I had done some scheming the night before. I was supposed

The champagne & wedding invitations

to give Janice her re-engagement ring (my youngest daughter came up with the terms "re-engagement and re-propose") at the end of the balloon ride when we landed for breakfast. When we had learned the flight might be canceled due to the high wind, we came up with plan B. We had put together a picnic breakfast complete with champagne, orange juice and wedding invitations. We set out the champagne flutes and the little boxes that Vera made with the wedding invitations in them. When the girls caught back up with us and saw the set up, they were intrigued. With Janice distracted by opening her box, I was able to get behind her, get the ring box out of my pocket, drop to one knee, and re-propose. I had a brief moment of panic when she did not answer me right away and

One of the monstrous dunes on the Namib Desert

looked at me rather strangely. After taking everything in, she eventually said "yes" and proceeded to have some champagne and orange juice in celebration. We spent the rest of the morning just being tourists and taking lots of pictures.

We left Le Mirage and the Namib Desert just about lunchtime on our way to Johann and Vera's beach house in Henties Bay. On the way back, we had an interesting experience. For you to appreciate the experience, I need to tell you that about seventy to eighty percent of the roads in Namibia are gravel roads. Well maintained, but gravel nonetheless, and we had already spent eight to ten hours bouncing around them. Keeping that in mind, we started hearing a clanking sound coming from under the right front of the Mercedes van were riding in. When we pulled over to investigate, we discovered that the pin that holds the front brake calipers together had broken, and the calipers and brake pads were freely bouncing along in the wheel well. When this happened, we were forty or fifty miles away from anything and had seen only two other cars all morning. When we tried our cell phones, there was no signal so I figured we were stuck for a while. I had forgotten **hints number 6 and 6a**, but Johann had not. He proceeded to take the calipers off, bleed the air out of the brake line, cap it off, and away we went on three breaks. With my limited mechanical ability, we may have still been sitting there.

Even with our delay, we arrived at the house just before dinner, and we unloaded and relaxed for a few minutes. When we caught our breath, we headed right back out to find a restaurant. During dinner, we made plans for the next two days. After two days, and a lot of road miles, we were all pretty much wiped out and everyone turned in early. When we woke up next morning, we were quite disappointed because the wind had followed us up the coast. We went out for just a little while so Johann could show us what a Namibian sandstorm is like. The town of Henties Bay is sandwiched between the desert and the ocean. When the wind blows, the sand in from the east there is nothing to stop it until it hits the ocean, unless there is a house or other structure in the way. When we drove by the eastern-most edge of town, two or more feet of sand had already piled up against western side of the houses. This was way more than we wanted

Sand build up in a court yard during a sandstorm

to be out in, so we headed back to the house.

After lunch, things calmed down a bit, so we headed up the coast a short way to the Cape Cross seal colony. This was one of the places that Janice really wanted to see and it turned out to be pretty neat. According to the informational plaques along the boardwalk, there were 250,000 seals here, and it sure smelled like it. The best way I could describe the smell would be to combine the smell of decaying animal matter, decaying fish, and the resulting matter produced by the seals eating fish. Much to my amazement, the girls did not seem to mind. They were talking, laughing, and taking pictures. There were seals as far as I could see in any direction, and I soon lost interest. The girls were not ready to go yet, so I kept myself busy looking out on the water to see if I could spot a shark looking for a snack, but all of the seals were lucky that afternoon.

On the way back, we stopped at one of the naturally occurring salt flats. These flat pans trapped salt water that washed into them and, through evaporation, large salt crystals formed. Everyone thought this was interesting and the girls went about looking for samples to take home. The largest one they found was about the size of a grapefruit. They also took a bag of loose salt to show Johann's daughter, Zoe, how to make ice cream in Ziploc bags. We had one more stop on the way back, and that was at the site of a shipwreck. North Carolina has the "Grave Yard of the Atlantic", and Namibia has the "Skeleton Coast", so we wanted to see how they stacked up against each other. While I can't remember a ship wreck off of the North Carolina coast in recent history, there were several very recent ones on the skeleton coast. One of the wrecks we stopped to look at was still actively being cut up for scrap. I guess the skeleton beat the ghost after all, at least in the current events category.

The morning of day four had us up early and heading to Swakopmund, or "Swakop" as the locals called it. Johann dropped us off downtown and went to see if he could find parts to repair the brakes. Swakop is a neat little town. After we had breakfast, we walked across the street and the girls did some shopping. From there, we visited the Swakopmund Museum. I was not really expecting a lot since this was a small town and, I thought it would be a small museum, but, boy was I wrong. The museum was very well put together and very informative. The first wing was all about the indigenous people. It described each group and then showed how some of the groups blended them into the current population. There were plenty of displays and artifacts from the early days of European settlement. These gave us a pretty good idea of what the early settlers lives were like. The next area had the natural resources of Namibia on display. Namibia has one of the world's richest and wide-ranging selections of minerals and gemstones anywhere. The wildlife of Namibia was well represented with a large collection of full size specimens. We spent a good chunk of the morning there and enjoyed every minute of it. Next, we stopped for something to drink and for ice cream. While we quenched our thirst and hunger, we made our way to the open-air market. We looked around there until Johann met up with us a short time later. He suggested another attraction, and we made our way to a museum dedicated to Namibia's vast gemstone, crystal, and mineral wealth. While we were there, I completed one of the first task dictated by our American, modified African wedding plan. I had to find something to mark my bride as mine and nobody else's. Kristine and Jessica helped me pick out an amethyst pendant set in silver with a silver chain to wear it on. I guess the African spirits took pity on me and let me find this combination, as amethyst is Janice's birthstone and it was our 25th or our Silver Anniversary.

After lunch, it was time to grant the wish of my youngest daughter Jessica, and that was to ride a camel in the desert. How Johann found or met this woman, I do not know, but she was a wonderful host and the girls had a wonderful time. When we got there, she took us aside and put a keffiyeh or traditional desert head covering on all of us. After the girls mounted their camels, I took the lead of the first camel and posed for pictures. I am not wild about having my picture taken, but I have to admit that this picture made for a pretty funny Christmas card. After the girls had their camel ride, it was time for another form of desert transportation, four wheelers. We rented some ATVs and headed out into the dunes. Our guide led us on a route that took us a good distance out into the desert. It was a little unnerving when we stopped and there was nothing but sand in every direction. There were no rocks, no plants, nothing but sand. It did not take much imagination to get a full dose of the despair anyone stranded in the desert must feel. As we made our way back, the view from the next-to-last dune was very cool. From the

The camel ride

4-Wheelers in the open desert

top of the dune, I could see sand and then the ocean. The desert literally stopped at the water's edge.

The next morning found our group on the way to Tualuka, Johann's five-star lodge in the mountains of the Outjo district. I had been there two years ago, and the experience of driving up to it left me speechless. I wanted to see if it had the same effect on the girls, so I turned around just to watch them. When you turn off the main road, the terrain is nothing but rocks and scrub. As you drive further into the valley, the vegetation becomes more lush and plentiful with the long, golden grass swaying in the afternoon sun. Even though it is in the middle of the winter, there is still thick, dormant vegetation. As you drive a little further you can see why, as you drop down into the dry bed of the Huab River. When there is water in this river, it is a massive body of water well over one hundred yards across in places. When we popped up out of the riverbed on the other side, the lodge came into view. It is built into the side of a mountain and blends in perfectly with its surroundings. Vera, Zoe, and Johann's parents, Vellies and Clarissa, were there to greet us. I felt like I had returned home after much too long an absence. As our luggage made its way to our chalets, I showed the girls around a little and pointed out the white flag that flew from the flagpole. I told them that when the white flag was raised in an African village it told everyone that a wedding was about to take place. That and that some poor guy had lost his battle to stay single, but I kept that thought to myself. When we all had changed and freshened up, we met back at the lodge, and the girls got better acquainted with the rest of the Veldsman family. I think it was somewhat difficult for my wife and kids to see this as a truly wild place in Africa, simply because of the level of luxury the camp lodge provided. Johann changed that in a heartbeat when he told them about walking between their chalets and the lodge after dark. He told them to stay on the elevated sidewalk cut into the kopje. When they asked why, he told them that the local elephants sometimes walked right up to the chalets to drink water and eat the flowers. If the girls startled the elephants, they could get very dangerous.

About an hour before dark, Johann piled us all in the Mercedes Unimog and took us on an evening game drive. I felt relaxed and at home in the bush and I think the girls liked it as well. The animals were cooperating, and the girls were giving their cameras a real workout as we made our way deeper into the bush. As we started to climb a kopje, I hoped we were headed to one of my favorite places on the property, a covered observation post perched on top of a kopje. As we made our way to the top, I noticed Vellies' land cruiser. As we walked in, a marvelous spread was waiting for us. There were plenty of makings for sundowners and several other treats. It was the perfect setting for my family's first sundowners in the African Bush. It was a fantastic evening, old friends getting reacquainted, new friendships forming and just enjoying a fantastic sunset. Later in the evening, the girls had their first dinner on fine china in the remote mountains of Namibia.

We scheduled a game drive for the morning. The girls were up early and excited. I didn't dare tell then that it had a dual purpose, the other being a scouting trip for my afternoon hunt. The girls wanted to see the mountain zebra, and so did I as it was my chosen quarry for this trip, and we needed to find out where they were. Johann knows this place well enough to drive it with his eyes closed, but he had been gone for close to a week, making a little reconnoitering necessary. You might be wondering how I got a hunt in on a family vacation. As it happens, it is a tradition for the groom to kill a goat or steer for the wedding feast. Through a little imagination and creative license, it did not take long for me to transform livestock into wild game. After riding for a while and seeing everything but zebra, we parked the Unimog and started uphill to a ridge that led over into another valley. There they were, grazing over on another ridge a hundred yards away. We hunkered down under some bush, and the girls had their cameras clicking away. I was glad that we were not too close and the zebra were unaware of our presence. If we did not spook them when we left, they would probably bed down somewhere close during the heat of the day and not move to far this afternoon. Since it was late morning and it was already hot, the girls did not seem to mind the suggestion to head back.

When Johann and I left that afternoon, the girls were getting ready to do some crafts with Zoe and then show her how to make ice cream in a Ziploc bag with the salt they saved from the beach. We left the girls to their own fun and we drove back toward where we had seen the zebra earlier that morning. We approached from a slightly different direction in an effort to stay down wind. Talk about **hints 6 and 6a**, the zebras were not even in the same zip code that we let them in this morning. We walked several miles and drove for a few more, but someone had warned the zebra that we were coming and they had left out for parts unknown. I made a mental note to question the girls when I got back to see if they had anything to do with the strange disappearance of the zebra. When we arrived back at the lodge that afternoon, the girls were returning from a game walk with Johnas. They had come across a herd of gemsbok and a large solitary kudu up on the side of a kopje. The thing that excited them the most was sneaking in on a family of warthogs and getting some good pictures. They had also seen another group of zebra, and that raised even more my level of suspicion of their involvement in the disappearance of the first group of zebra.

Dinner was an engagement party of sorts. Everyone, including myself, was caught off guard with the engagement gift that Vera presented to Janice. According to the local custom, the bride was supposed to be given some snacks and treats wrapped in a white cloth. The cloth Vera presented to Janice was a fine linen tablecloth, custom embroidered with zebras and African scenery. It was absolutely beautiful, and both of us were very appreciative. Afterwards, we had a few more cocktails and sat down to dinner. Since I had failed to bring in a zebra, Vera had made up for my shortcomings by taking some zebra that a previous hunter had taken and made kabobs. I had not seen kabobs cooked on a rotisserie before, but there are a lot of things in Africa that I have not seen before. The skewers fit into a wheel, which, in turn, fit onto a spit, which ended up over an open fire. Anything slow cooked over an open fire is bound to be delicious, and this was no exception. Baked potatoes, red cabbage, fresh bread, and a host of other decadent dishes made for a wonderful meal.

After dinner, Janice was supposed to prove her worthiness to marry me by passing a test. I won't go into the original African ceremonial details, but we decided to substitute a series of questions instead. Some months back, I sent Vera a bunch of gag questions for her to give to people to ask. For instance, one of them was, "How could a girl that graduated from the University of North Carolina put up with someone that graduated from North Carolina State University". I thought that the Veldsman family was to be the inquisitors, but Vera gave my girls the questions instead. All I can say is that I was quite relieved that some of them mysteriously disappeared. Anyway, all of us had a good time, and we closed out the evening with a champagne toast. Then, it was off to bed.

5:00 am is too dog gone early to get up on your wedding day, but I was going to try and track down Mr. Zebra one more time. Johann and I had a quick cup of coffee and headed to the truck. We were going to try the other side of the property and wanted to be there before daybreak. I could bore you with a lot of "we went up this side and down the other", but the plain and simple truth is that we could not find any zebra anywhere. We found their tracks and where they had been, but we had no idea where they were now. We saw gemsbok and kudu. We found a leopard kill. We found just about everything but what we were looking for. In no time at all, we had used up the small part of the morning we were allotted, and we dutifully headed back to the lodge. After all, there was going to be a wedding today.

We made it back for breakfast with everyone else at the appointed hour of 9:00 am, and I proceeded to thoroughly enjoy myself. I did not realize that I had worked up that big an appetite. Vera shooed us away from the lodge so she could start decorating. The girls mentioned wanting to see elephants, so Johann took us down river to see if we could find any. The elephants made themselves scarce, so Johann regaled the girls with his knowledge of the bush. He told us stories of trees that were sacred to the indigenous people, what plants were edible and which were poisonous, and much more. The one that the girls liked the most was how to judge the size of an elephant without ever seeing it. Even though the local elephants were not around, there were plenty of tracks. He showed us how to measure an elephant's track, double that, and that was approximately the height of the elephant at the shoulder. The track he measured belonged to an elephant that was nine feet or so tall. Pretty cool huh?

When we got back to the lodge for lunch, we found that Vera had banished Janice from the lodge until the ceremony and that we would be having lunch on the veranda of our chalet. After lunch, the Veldsmans continued to shower Janice with gifts. Vellies brought down a selection of huge silver topaz stones and told Janice to pick out one for her Silver Anniversary. Vera and Zoe gave her a basket of bath soaps and oils, so she could pamper herself that afternoon. The visits were short as there were still items to attend to and decorations to put up, so they said goodbye, leaving us to have a pleasant and relaxing afternoon.

Six and 6a reared their ugly heads again, and I was starting to get tired of them doing so. The local pastor that had agreed to perform the ceremony was lost and could not find his way to the lodge, so Johann was going to go to try to find him. While he was gone, I decided to spring my last surprise on Janice as a distraction. Way back when we were first married, we had a seven o'clock formal wedding, complete with tuxedos with cutaway tails. Since I had told her the dress was formal bush attire, I had a seamstress make two formal bush jackets with cutaway tails. One was for me and the other was for Johann, since he had agreed to be my best man. She was most surprised that I had gone to all the trouble to have the coats made just for the wedding. That is when I made my mistake. I explained that the coats were dual-purpose and pointed out that the tails were removable. Without the tails, the jacket then became plain safari attire. I should have kept my mouth shut and quit while I was ahead. She still appreciated the gesture, but I had taken some of the sparkle out of it by pointing out the duality of the jacket.

Six and 6a were still going strong because now not only could we not find the preacher, we had lost Johann as well. In the meantime, Johann's mother, Clarissa, had agreed to fill in for the preacher if necessary, and I was giving her a "Readers Digest" version of the ceremony that Vera and I had worked out. While I was doing that, Johann had found a place with cellular reception and Vera had told him to stop looking for the preacher and to return home so things could start on time. After filling in Clarissa on the ceremony, I headed back to dress and pose for some pictures. Vellies is also quite a good photographer and had agreed to help us out with the picture taking. He posed us in various places around the lodge, giving the pictures different effects. Some that he took in the flower garden were like normal wedding pictures; others with the bush in the background gave the appearance of us being in the middle of nowhere. After we were done taking pictures, all we could do was wait. Johann got back a short while later and, as soon as he was able to catch his breath and change clothes, we could start the wedding.

Since guys really can't really describe a wedding the way our spouses remember it, I am going to use my wife's words as I found them in her journal of the trip.

Johann came and walked me from the cottage up the hill to the lodge. I didn't know what to expect, because I hadn't been allowed to see anything. It was beautiful, candles and flowers everywhere and white bunting on the railings. All the staff was there with all the Veldsman family. They made an altar out of the reception counter and Clarissa was there to perform the ceremony. She did a beautiful job and made me cry as she told the stages of marriage. The staff sang for us and I was very touched by their kindness. After the vows, we gathered for cocktails and we asked the staff to join us. The dinner table was beautifully set with place cards and menus that Vera, Clarissa, and Zoe had made. The color scheme was bronze and

Springbuck roasting on the spit

The table setting for the wedding dinner

burgundy. For dinner, we had springbok that Vellies had roasted on a spit over the fire, vegetables, and salad. The desserts were amazing, strawberry torts, and cheesecake with chocolate truffles on top. We finished the evening sitting by the fire.

I do not know what I can possibly add to that other than to thank her for saying "I do."

The next morning found us off on another long dive that would take us to Etosha National Park. Etosha is a really neat place. We stayed at one of its main resorts, Okaukuejo. The resort is laid out in a horseshoe shape, with offices and the restaurant at the base and cabins down each side. The whole thing is fenced to keep the people in and the animals out. In the center of the horseshoe is a water hole to attract the wildlife in close for easy viewing. After we checked in, and looked around for a while, then Johann took us on a game drive. The quantity of animals in the park was quite phenomenal. You could look in any direction and see an animal of some sort. One of Janice's favorites was the giraffes. Johann eased the jeep along and we were able to get close enough for her to get some incredible pictures. I have no idea of how many memory cards she filled up as she snapped away for the rest of the afternoon, but the camera was never away from her face for very long. We saw every animal that the girls wanted to see but one, the king of beasts. We could not find the Panthera Leo, no matter where we looked, and we looked in every hidey-hole that Johann knew about. We were running out of daylight and, since guests are not allowed outside the resort after dark, we headed back. On the way back, we decided to take one of the night tours that the park offered. These tours are touted as being able to find lions for night viewing.

Dinner passed quickly as all of us were excited about the upcoming nighttime viewing. We had some time to spare between dinner and our tour, so we headed to the water hole to see what was there. Etosha has the water hole set up right. There are rows of elevated seats on either flank, with a single row of seating alternating with standing room directly in front. After dark, the whole thing is lit up like a Friday night high school football game. Anything that comes to the waterhole is easy to see and, with the right kind of camera, you can get some good pictures. I was glad we decided to stop by because there were some elephants and white rhinoceroses that came in for a drink. We had seen both species in a zoo before, but there is something quite different when they are the ones on the outside, and you are the one fenced in. We sat for a while almost mesmerized by the coming and goings of so many different species of animals.

Luckily, someone noticed the time and we headed over to where we were supposed to meet our driver. He was there waiting for us and the other guest who had signed up for the tour. The vehicle was a form of the land rover that had the driver's seat and six or so rows of bench seats behind that. The sides were open from about halfway up the seats to the roof to provide easy viewing. We all piled in and, in short order, we were outside of the gates, and we headed off to find some lions. All was going well and the guide was doing a good job of pointing out the various nocturnal residents of Etosha, until we reached the first location to stop and see if we could hear the lions. Before he restarted the truck, he asked if there were any questions. I had to open my big mouth and ask him what type of rifle he carried if the lions tried to get into the truck. He responded that no firearms were allowed inside the park. I then asked if the lions wanted in the truck how he planned to keep them out. His answer was that he could not keep them out, but that he never head of a lion trying to take a ride in a truck. He then cranked the truck and we drove off to the next location. As we drove off, all of the guests sort of looked at each other with wide eyes and nobody said a word. We temporarily forgot about the lions because of the cold. The temperature was in the mid-thirties and breeze made it downright cold. Someone finally noticed that there were some blankets stowed in a net at the roofline. We pulled them down and they did a nice job of cutting the wind and warming us up enough to remember the lions. Remembering the lions was as close as we got to them on the tour, as they remained hidden elsewhere in the park. When we got back, we wanted one more look at the water hole before we turned in. As we approached the water hole, it was buzzing with excitement. When we got closer, it turns out that a large male lion had been sitting at the water hole for a while and was now making his exit via stage left. I am really starting not to like **6 and 6a.**

After breakfast, we headed out of the park, but on a roundabout route that gave us one last game drive. **6 and 6a** must have slept in because we caught a lucky break when we spotted a very old solitary elephant bull. He was about sixty yards away and feeding and moving slowly toward us. The cameras were in overdrive once again as the old tusker got closer and closer. Everyone knows elephants are big but until you get really close to one, you just do not get the whole picture. If you can imagine looking out the window of a Jeep Cherokee and being on eye level with this guy's knee, you can begin to picture how big he was. I know he had to see us, but he walked up to about twelve feet from us before he got too close for comfort and we took our leave. After our up close and personal experience with the elephant, we had a leisurely drive

What an elephant looks like from less than 10 yards

to the park gate. We saw lots more game, but the old bull continued to dominate the conversation.

Our next stop was about two hours away. It was a ranch called Ermo. Johann had worked out an arrangement that allowed his clients to hunt there and we were slated to try for a springbok or wildebeest tomorrow morning. We took some back roads to increase the odds of seeing more wildlife. It paid off when we came across a group of giraffe, the first ones I had seen in Africa outside of the park. It was an interesting sight, seeing their heads above the telephone lines. The wildlife activity had slowed down and we all were sort of lost in our thoughts when Johann hit the brakes and stopped the car. He got us out and pointed out a huge puff adder that had been warming itself by soaking up the sun shining down on the road. This snake was so fat; I wondered how it could ever move fast enough to bite anything. When we were ready to leave, Johann showed us just how fast it could move by throwing a small rock at it, and it disappeared into the brush at the side of the road. If you had blinked, you would have missed it. It was that fast. The rest of the trip was uneventful except for seeing lots of springbok and a huge eland as we got closer to the Ermo.

Ermo itself was interesting. It was a working farm and a guesthouse. We were the only guests that night and had the full attention of the staff. We all got along famously. I was able to try something new for dinner. Gnu was the main dish, and I had never had the opportunity to try it before. If you are not familiar with Gnu, it is another name for the wildebeest, and I found it quite tasty. Several exchange students from Germany working there and their company made dinner quite interesting. They were around Kristine's age and they did not speak much English. Kristine spoke French as a second language and no German. It was obvious both groups were happy to see someone new that was about their own age. I found it quite entertaining watching them communicate without being able to speak each other's language. If there is a way to do it, teenage girls will figure it out. I spent most of the evening talking to Obie (pronounced like "hobby" without the H). The ranch borders Etosha, and he was having problems with the lions killing his livestock. He had killed two in the last week. It boggled my mind that someone out tending cattle and came across lions on a somewhat regular basis acted as if it was no big deal. I would have been in a constant state of paranoia that they might see me before I saw them. The fact that he and his wife, Stephie, had younger children that were probably adept at getting out from under a parent's watchful eye would have driven me insane if they had been my kids. I guess growing up with it desensitizes you to things like that. They would probably be a nervous wreck if their kid had been playing in a typical American neighborhood, worrying about them being hit by a car. To each goes their own set of worries.

The winds were howling when I got up to start my hunt, but I was going anyway. I was having fun doing the family vacation thing, but I wanted to hunt and I was going to do it, come gentle breeze or gale-force winds. Johann and I just shook our heads when we saw each other at breakfast. He said it didn't look good, but we were going to give it our best shot. I was wondering if the wind was going to affect the springbuck and wildebeest and make them disappear like the zebras I had been looking for earlier. As it turned out, the animals were hiding in plain sight. They had picked locations that were six to eight hundred yards away from anything. They could see anything coming from any direction and do it from a long ways off. We tried crawling to get within range, and tried to look like one of them by holding the shooting sticks up like antlers, and even pretended to be working on the fence, and nothing was working. It was going to be a long shot or no shot. I knew the bullet drop on my rifle and I eventually got to within about 300 yards of a decent springbuck ram. The wind was howling and pushing my rifle around on the sticks. I finally got into a position that I thought I could brace myself in and started to concentrate on the shot. I guesstimated that I should hold two body lengths in front of the ram to allow for windage. When I got comfortable and settled in, I squeezed off a shot just as the wind gusted I saw a poof of dust kick up two feet behind the ram. The ram had no idea of where the shot came from, so he simply ran a few feet and stopped. I thought about trying another shot and allowing for more windage, but quickly thought better of it. This type of shooting was way beyond my ability and I felt foolish for trying a shot in the first place. As things stood, I had an unwounded animal and I could walk away clean. Walking away was the best choice, so it was what we did.

If the hunting was not going to cooperate, Johann decided to show me around the place instead. Once I got out of hunting mode and could pay attention, I noticed the farm was really a pretty place. It had varying terrain and easy access because of the farm roads that crisscrossed the property. I had just started to enjoy the scenery when the breaks of the truck locked up and we came screeching to a stop. Johann had seen a group of wildebeest on the other side of a small clump of trees. He thought we could get close enough for a good shot. Getting quickly back into hunting mode, I uncased and reloaded my rifle. We eased out of the truck, got low, and eased our way toward the trees. It took a while, because the howling wind kept the herd moving a little at a time and we kept having to stop and adjust our route to the trees. We ended up having to crawl the last little bit to get to our hide but it was worth it. When we got there, I got that lucky feeling that happens when things start to go right. I got the feeling when I looked up at the tree. There was a fork in it that was the perfect height for a rifle rest if I was in a sitting position. I eased into position as Johann looked over the heard to see if there were any good bulls. When he confirmed that there were several good bulls in the group, I knew that my luck had changed.

Yes sir, all we had to do was wait for one of the bulls to move away, and I was going to get me a nice wildebeest. Yep, just wait for one to move just a little ways off. Any minute now, that really nice bull is going to step out into the clear and, bang, I've got him. The pendulum that told me my luck had changed was now swinging back so hard the other way that if it had hit me I would have been out cold. The wind had those critters so nervous that they had bunched up against each other tight as a tick. They were not doing anything but moving a few feet one way or the other and they were doing that in unison. My hopes were fading fast as the minutes went by, but I was determined to stick things out and make my own good luck. It was less than a minute after I gave myself that little pep talk when any hopes of taking a wildebeest bull were summarily and thoroughly dashed against the hard ground that I had been sitting on for the last few minutes. The wind that had been steadily blowing from one direction all morning long, inexplicably decided to shift to our backs. It took less than half a second to get to the wildebeest and, when it did, they decided they wanted to be elsewhere. We tried to follow them for a while by weaving in and out of the trees and low brush but the wildebeest knew we were there. Every time we closed the distance, it was only a few seconds until they opened it back up. We were beat and we knew it. It was time to give up the chase for today, but there is always tomorrow.

Johann had a treat for us on the way back to Tualuka. He knew some people that ran a cheetah rescue and we were going to stop by for a visit. When we got there, was no one in sight, so we waited. It took a few minutes for our welcoming committee to show up and when it did, it was in the form of a young giraffe. He walked right up to us and bent down wanting to be petted. We looked at Johann and he shrugged and

The friendly giraffe

Jessica & Kristine at the cheetah rescue

said that he had not seen it before. When no one was brave enough to pet it, the youngster walked over to Janice and proceeded to try to stick his nose down her shirt. She was forced to pet him in self-defense and, before long, everyone had taken a turn scratching his head or neck. We all thought this was cool, but the best was yet to come. A few minutes after the giraffe became bored with us, one of the owners noticed we were there, and invited us into the compound. Once we were inside the gate, two adult cheetahs and a very rambunctious cub immediately welcomed us in. The o.k. was given to pet them, and everyone wanted to give it a try. I sat back for a minute just to watch Janice and the girls pet these large cats. Out of all the memories I have of Africa, this one will always be among my favorites. The looks on their faces was priceless and I would not take anything for it. When I took my turn, I was surprised at the coarseness of their fur. Their coat was short and stiff, almost like a scrub brush. I have always been enamored with the big cats, and being up close and personal was a special treat.

We made it back to the lodge early evening and were delighted that Vera's parents were able to join us for the evening. After ten days in country, it was nice to have nothing to do for the evening and just be able to relax and visit. I had met Vera's father several times before and was looking forward to catching up over a dinner and a few sundowners.

Day eleven started early and the wind was still howling. Johann, Johnas, and I were searching desperately searching for a zebra. The wind was doing us no favors. While it covered our noise as we walked, it had made all of the game more skittish. Add heat and the combination of the two, made hunting extremely tough. The wind was taking away one of their primary defenses; they could not hear danger approaching. Most of the animals we found were sticking to the shady spots in small isolated pockets out of the wind. When we adapted our hunting style to looking for and investigating these spots, we started seeing more game. There just happened to be no zebra among the animals we found. This was frustrating Johann more than me. We went to place after place and there were just no zebra to be found. In an effort to lighten the mood, I asked if he had lost any radios lately. He said, no, and then asked why I wanted to know that. My response was that, if he had, I could understand why we were not seeing any zebra. I could tell by the puzzled look on his face that he needed a little more information to get my feeble attempt at humor. I then added that the only way that I could figure that the zebra were staying hidden was if someone was giving them updates on where we were headed and the zebra were moving before we got there. He evidently did not think that I was too funny because the only response I got was a rolling of the eyes, a grunt of some kind, and a quickening of the pace as we headed to our next spot. We spent the entire day traveling from spot to spot and looking everywhere in between, but Mr. Zebra was nowhere to be found.

Sundowners and dinner made up for a poor day's hunting. Jan and Mariesje du Plesses were joining us and it would be good to get reacquainted with them. Jan and Mariesje are good friends with Johann And Vera. Jan is a PH also and bears some of the responsibility for getting Johann interested in becoming a PH. I have had the pleasure of hunting with Jan and would do so again in a heartbeat. While he is on the hunt, he is one of the most intense and focused hunters I have ever seen. His personality outside of that is quite the opposite, he is light-hearted and can be quite a practical joker. Anyway, he and Mariesje are a lot of fun to be around, and I was glad that Janice and the girls got the chance to meet them. We had a wonderful evening swiping stories of our adventures since we had last seen each other and reliving a few old tales as well.

Today is the last day at Tualuka. It is now or never as the old saying goes. I am optimistic as Johann tells me that he has a new strategy to try today. There is only one other place to look that we have not tried yet. Instead of looking in small hidey-holes as we had been doing, we are going to check the leeward side of the ridge tops. Today Vellies would be joining our little trio and facilitate our mountain top strategy. Johann's plan was to go up the kopje, with the wind at our back, and peek over the ridge from either the far right or far left side. Hopefully, the zebra would be somewhere in the middle forty to sixty yards down from the top of the ridge. If they were not on the first ridge, we would hike over the mountain and Vellies would drive the Unimog around to the other side. That would keep us from having to backtrack and wasting valuable time. Johann must have been in a hurry to see if his plan was going to work because he wasted no time in getting to the top of the first ridge. I was just about to catch up with him when he suddenly froze, hit the ground, and motioned for me to do the same. We had found our quarry. We backed off down the other side a little and regrouped. There was a small herd, and he thought there were a few subordinate males in the group. He had already told me that unless the lead stallion looked to be past his prime, we would be targeting younger males. If we took the younger stallions out, that removed some of the dominate stallion's stress of constantly being challenged and having to fight to keep his position. That led to less stress on the mares and better breeding success. By using this model, the population of zebras on his concession had more than tripled in just three years.

In order for us to get into a location where I could take a shot at the zebras, we had to work our way around the back of the ridge and then climb up to a small spot on top that had a few trees. Hopefully, the trees would give us a little cover and I could get a shot off before the herd winded us. We climbed as quickly and as silently as we could. Johann was glassing as I worked my way into a position to see and perhaps get a shot. A few seconds after I had gotten into position, he pointed out the animal I was to take. He told me to be quick because the wind at our backs would blow our scent to them in no time at all. I was trying my best to comply with his request and I did what I warned you against in **hint number thirty-nine,**

I shot before I was ready and I muffed the shot. The zebra moved only a short way to a position behind a small clump of trees. It evidentially could not tell where the shot originated from. I was ready with my follow-up shot, but I had a bad angle. Johann said he had a shot, and I told him to take it. He had tried to take out the hip but just missed the bone. The race was then on. The zebra had separated from the herd, so I was able to keep him in sight. We were going down a steep grade full of loose rocks. Moving at all was treacherous, but we had to keep up with the zebra. He moved into a shooting lane and I said I had a shot. When Johann said I could take it, I did what could best be described as a modified slide into third base. I was sliding downhill with my right foot underneath me and my left foot in front. When I stopped, I raised my left knee for a rest, lined up the zebra and took the shot. This time the hit was

much better, and I knew that I had my
zebra even though it was not off its feet
yet. The animal had at least reduced its
speed to a slow walk. I was ready with
another shot when Johann said to hold
up, keep it in the scope, but do not
shoot. He said the zebra was making our
recovery job much easier with every step
it took down the side of the mountain.
We watched until it stopped on a small
almost level piece of ground and Johann

Johann Veldsman & myself with the ever elusive zebra

said to anchor it. With one last report from the 9.3, it was over. The zebra
was on the ground and my hunt was over. I was mad at myself for my
poor first shot, but I felt a little redeemed by some better follow-up shots.

After we worked our way down to the zebra, I was glad that Johann
knew and practiced my mantra of "what your brain does not do your
back has to". By allowing the zebra to descend under its own power, we
saved ourselves a lot (and I mean a lot) of work. The stallion ended up on
a small ridge top a little more than halfway down the mountain. Johann
told me to sit tight while he went to go get the Unimog. I proceeded
to start clearing away some of the rocks and brush that would hamper
taking pictures, and then started clearing a path the rest of the way down
the mountain. I had figured out all by myself that the only way to get the
zebra in the truck was to put it on a heavy-duty tarp that Johann had in
the back of the vehicle and slide it down the mountain. I had worked up a
pretty good sweat and went back up top to get the water bottle out of my
daypack. I was just about to resume clearing when I heard the Unimog's
engine grunting and groaning. I walked over to the front right corner and
looked over the edge and, low and behold, here came Johann driving the
Unimog up a grade that I would not have been comfortable walking up.

This vehicle was running over bushes, trees, rocks, virtually anything that got in its way. In another minute, he would be up on top with the truck and we would be able to load from here. I have never in my life been so glad at not having been seen working hard. I am as sure that they all would have gotten a good laugh at my naiveté concerning the capabilities of the Unimog, as I am sure that they will laugh when they read this. At least I will not have to be there in person. When all of the pictures were taken, it was off to the skinning shed, and to have a quiet celebratory lunch with the girls.

The girls wanted one last game drive, and Johann was happy to oblige. We eased our way through the veldt and the game seemed to want to cooperate with us. Maybe they were just happy that the wind had died down to a dull roar and they could move about as they wanted. The girls had become quite proficient at spotting game and were finding the animals without Johann having to point them out. I had finally gotten my spotting ability back and found a few of them myself. Johann timed our arrival at the observation deck to coincide perfectly with the time the sun kissed the horizon. This was our last sundowner at Tualuka. I was already starting to miss the place. There was no time for sadness, though, as I was in a place that I loved, with people that meant the world to me. Best of all, my wife and children were there with me to share in the experience. As we sipped our sundowners, laughed and made plans for the future, all was indeed right with my little corner of the world. On the way back to the lodge for dinner, Johann stopped the Unimog and gave us an astronomy lesson. The Southern Cross is easy enough to pick out, and I knew its orientation was close to north and south. What I did not know was that you took the small stars to the side and extended the line they made with the north-south axis of the Southern Cross until the lines intersected, and that was true south. He also showed us the largest constellation in the southern hemisphere, Scorpio.

The morning of our thirteenth day found us up early, not for any type of fun or even hunting. We were up early for the most horrible thing you have to do on safari, packing to go home. Even though I had one night in Omuzire and one in Windhoek, I knew this was the beginning of the end of our trip and I dreaded it. As a diversion, Johann had arranged for us to tour a Himba village on the way to Omuzire. We were met by a guide when we arrived, and he told us a little of the history of the tribe and village on the short walk to it. The fact that people actually still lived this way is something that I had not spent much time thinking about before. Their huts are still made in the same manner as they have been for hundreds of years, from a manure and mud mixture that is applied to a stick frame. Even with the primitive surroundings, they did have a few modern connivances. These were so prized that they were hung out on display in a tree by the hut. The iron skillet and the saucepan clanked together in the breeze like a homemade wind chime. Everyone seemed to be happy. The adults were smiling and the children were running around laughing and playing. I was the one that was out of place. After I had a moment to think about it, I realized the poverty was not responsible for my being uncomfortable. It was the naked children and the topless women that were the reason for my discomfort. Before anyone accuses me of being a prude, I defy any father to stand around with a group of topless women in the presence of his wife and teenage daughters without feeling strange. I do not know why, but the whole time we were there, I had to fight the urge to study every cloud in the sky and whistle. Janice and the kids enjoyed the visit and wanted to learn all about of their customs. One of the things they were curious about was the red color of the women's skin. The women make and use a type of makeup from a powdered red stone and fat to coat their bodies and protect their skin. We also learned that it is also more important for the female ankle to be covered than any other body part. The women are quite skilled as jewelry makers and, at the end of our visit, all of their wares were put out in the center of the village for our inspection. Janice and the girls bought several pieces as mementos of their visit.

After we left the village, we drove for a while and then stopped for lunch. Johann asked if we were hungry and, when we answered in the affirmative, he suggested we try the hamburgers, as they were large and very good. The girls and I ordered hamburgers and anxiously awaited our lunch. When the plates came out, the hamburger was as large as the plate. Honest-to-gosh, these hamburgers were almost twelve inches across, and, with bun, fixings and patty, were three inches thick. I looked at Johann and his only comment was "I told you they were big" and "you said that you were hungry". I could tell by the look on his face that he had purposely not told us how big just to play a joke on us. I decided to show him, by golly. I would eat the whole thing. I ordered another beverage and set upon my task with a vengeance. A little past the halfway point, I started to slow down. At the two-thirds point, I was starting to think I could be in trouble. At the three quarter point, I caught my second wind and thought the finish line was attainable. About two bites after that, I knew I had made a mistake. Not only did I not finish it, but I did succeed in making myself miserable for the rest of the afternoon.

When we got to camp, we had a little time to look around and get settled in before the late afternoon game drive. We were sitting around the fire pit inside the boma when Janice sent me after her coat because we were due to leave on the drive soon. Of course, the girls said "get ours too, daddy", so I was off to fetch everyone's coats. It is a good thing I got back when I did because I returning at that precise time probably saved a life. Just as I was making my way through the entrance to the boma after retrieving everyone's coats, an Egyptian cobra was blocking my path. I took a quick step and brought my boot down just behind its head, breaking its neck. As soon as I did that, everyone broke out in laughter. I guess it was to relieve the tension and to deal with the shock at my heroic action. Their laughter had dissipated some by the time I had handed everyone their jacket, so I asked why they were still laughing. They made up some cock and bull story about that shortly after I left Johann's staff had brought the snake that THEY had killed to show everyone. Then

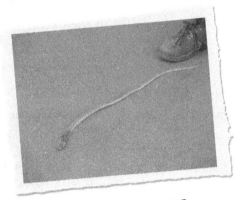

The cobra that I saved everyone from

Johann had the idea to place it across the path to see what I would do and that when I came in I had stepped on it without seeing it and kept right on walking. I personally think that sometimes, in order to cope with fear, that people's minds do strange things and sometimes make you believe things that are just not true. Anyway, that is how I remember the event. They were lucky that I could see to step on the snake at all, with a double arm full of coats and sweatshirts.

All seven of us piled into the land cruiser and headed out for our last game drive. After riding around for a while, we headed toward a kopje that Johann uses as an observation and scouting point. I figured that he was just going to show the girls where we started a lot of our stalks from. When we arrived, he stopped, grabbed a cooler, and said, "Everyone follow me to the top". Now, this kopje was rugged and had kicked my backside more than once trying to keep up with Johann in getting to the top. I mentioned that I thought the path we took was not going to work. He just looked at me, gave me an evil smile, and said, "I'll take them the easy way". "What, there is an easy way up from here? How come I never knew about an easy way?" He just turned and headed around the corner. I guess he was still in shock from that whole cobra thing and

I should probably cut him some slack. We all made it to the top and, when he opened the cooler and handed out sundowners, I quickly forgot about his temporary memory lapse. Heck, even I forget things from time to time. Everyone found himself or herself a place to sit and enjoyed the view and his or her sundowner. We all were doing our own thing, relaxing, looking for animals, taking pictures, or just contemplating life in general. We could see for tens of miles in any direction, all the way to the next mountain range. As the sun eased its way behind them and night began to fall, my mind started to wander as it often does to the Africa I have read so many books about, wondering just how much it had changed in the last century and how much it would change in the next. In the end, I decided that Africa was changing on "African Time", slower and at a more deliberate pace. I was glad that Africa was not changing at the breakneck speed the rest of my world seemed to be. I was glad that I could bring my children here to see her as she is now, and maybe start that spark in them that would bring them back some day. I was happy and refused to acknowledge the fact that this was our last night in the bush, and tomorrow it was back to Windhoek, and then home.

We had to leave our lofty perch before darkness completely fell and head back to the truck. Just as we all on board and were ready to leave, Johann turned on the head lights. Something long and black slithered across the road about thirty feet in front of us. Johann grabbed his rifle, jumped out of the truck and headed towards it. I am thinking mamba because he killed one close to here a few weeks ago. When he got closer, instead of

Kristine and Jessica's last sunset in the bush

aiming the rifle to shoot the snake, he reaches down and grabs it. In about half a heartbeat, the snake turns and comes at Johann. Great, I think to myself, since I got away with saving everyone from a snake a few hours ago, he is going to try to do it now. Luckily, the snake missed Johann and he let it go at the same time. It went back across the road and disappeared. As Johann started back towards the truck, Vera finally got her breath back and yelled, "Have you lost your mind?!!!" He said, "you have to see this", got back into the truck and pulled down the road and under a tree beside where the snake had disappeared. He turned around and informed us that the snake was a boa, and pretty one at that, and, if we wanted to see it, to look up. When the words "look up" sunk in to everyone's psyche, everyone wanted out of the truck. "Sit still and look up", he said again, "It isn't going anywhere". Once I located it, the snake did look as if it was

no longer worried about us and appeared to be just sitting there. Janice finally remembered her camera and took a few pictures. She finally managed to convince Johann that she had taken enough and for him to feel free to leave at any time.

The boa up a tree

As we were descending the last few feet of the kopje, we noticed several vehicles and people with flashlights moving slowly from the road into the bush. When we got a little closer, Vera recognized her father's truck and we stopped to investigate. It turns out that one of his employees had gone missing. At the end of the day, the missing man had stepped into the bush to relieve himself and simply disappeared. No one had heard or seen anything. It was unknown if he had found a snake, became disoriented or lost, something else had found him. The man had been dressed in light work clothes and now that sun was down, he would be getting very cold. On the way back to camp, I wondered how many people just disappeared in Africa, never to be seen again. This person did eventually turn up. It was about four days and fifty miles away. It turned out that he had run out of some kind of medicine and neglected to tell anyone about it. Without it, he suffered from some form of dementia. He was very lucky that he turned up at all. Africa is not always so kind and forgiving.

All of us had a very nice dinner that night. Vera combined my favorite, gemsbok, with Kristine's favorite, a feta cheese stuffing, for our last dinner. She cuts a slit in the side of a thick steak that was more the size of a roast, then she stuffs it with feta cheese, and a heavy cream sauce made with onions and bacon. She could not have picked a better meal for last evening in camp. After dinner, I poured myself one last glass of wine and joined everyone else around the fire. Instead of the Veldsman family and a guest, there were now two families sitting around the fire. It meant a great deal to me to be able to share this with my wife and children. It was important for them to be sitting at the same spot where Africa first infected me, so much so that I will always want to come back. It was important to me that two families came together and became friends. Most importantly, it is important that my wife and daughters have had a little taste of what changed me into what I am today. I do not know that they will ever pick up a rifle and follow me on a hunt. If not, that is ok. I do know, however, that a little piece of Africa has gotten to them, and they will be forever be the better for it.

On the way back to Windhoek, we were able to stop and visit with Sylvia and Otjwarongo Taxidermy for a short while. I had some crazy idea that if Janice could get a look at a trophy room done right, that she might change her opinion about them. Boy was I mistaken. While she liked the work, she reiterated her earlier comments about where my trophies could go when we got home. Anyway, it was nice to get a visit in. After we got to Windhoek, we spent the rest of the day doing something that almost all women like to do, shop. I was there simply to tote packages and dispense currency, and that was ok. I was just happy to see that all three of them had shaken off their fatigue and melancholy before we arrived at the first store. It was a most miraculous recovery. We did it all, covering a lot of shops and a lot of ground. We shopped at a local craft market, clothing stores, jewelry stores, and I am sure there are a few I missed. I am just glad they had some fun and found some treasures to take home with them, things that will hopefully jog a few memories loose on occasional, or maybe just trigger a smile.

After shopping, we checked into a B&B for a little rest and some cleaning up. Johann promised to take us to his favorite restaurant, the Cattleman Ranch Steakhouse for supper. The food is very good and pork ribs I had were excellent, and we all chowed down on them as we had our last dinner in Africa. Back at the B&B, the girls mentioned that they could not wait to get home for some Chinese food or Mexican food. They do not have too much longer to wait. Tomorrow afternoon, they will board a plane to take them back home. Me, I am headed to Zimbabwe. It is time to try something new and unfamiliar. What, you may ask? Well, that is another story.

I did not add this story to try to get you to take your family along on your first safari. That was not my intention at all, but if you would like to do so, it is certainly within your reach. I really just wanted to show you the broad spectrum of things that are available to do in Africa. It does not matter if it is a first-time plains game hunt, a hunt for dangerous game, a family vacation, or any combination of the above, you can do it. If that little spark has taken root in the back of your mind, do some investigating. Maybe you can get to grow into a bonfire.

CHAPTER TWELVE
Lists and Forms

The following list is a combination of lists given to me by Rick Wilks of Wilks' Safari Adventures, Johann Veldsman of Shona Hunting Adventures. It also has a few items of mine thrown in for good measure.

Qty	Item	Notes
Clothing		
1	Jacket	Light to mid-weight, windproof, and sized to fit over layers.
1	Sweater	Polar fleece or other lightweight insulating material
5	Shirts	3 long sleeve, one short sleeve, and one "T"
4	Pants	3 long and one pair of shorts
4pr	Underwear	
1	Camp Wear	Set of casual clothing for wear in and around camp
2pr	Boots	Well-broken-in – to switch daily to allow the boot to dry out.
3pr	Hiking Socks	Smart wool or other wicking / cushioning type
1	Camp shoes	To give your feet a break from your boots.
2pr	Athletic Socks	
1	Gators	Keeps debris out of short / ankle boots

1	Silk or Wicking Undershirt	Base layer or sleep shirt at night
1pr	Gloves	Leather or light insulating
1	Stocking Cap	
1	Wide Brimmed Hat	A wide brimmed hat can be a pain in thick brush. You might opt for a ball cap. Or take both.

Gear

1	Flashlight	Bright, 50+ lumens with extra batteries
1	Toiletries	Soap, shampoo, body wash, deodorant, etc., all unscented
1	Sunglasses	Extra pair recommended
1	Rifle(s)	With scope, back-up rifle with scope recommended
1	Gun Case	Airline approved hard case (or bow case if bow hunting)
1	Gun Case	Soft case for transporting rifle in safari truck
1	Cleaning kit	Including gun wipes
1	Binoculars	7-10 power is best
	Ammunition	40-60 rounds per gun up to 11 lbs
	Scope Covers	To protect scopes in open safari truck
1	Lens Pen	
1	Bore sight	Laser type preferred.
1	Day Pack	
1	Ear Plugs	
1	Pocket Knife	Or multi tool. A large hunting knife is unnecessary.
1	Camera	Include extra memory cards, batteries, or charger
	Small Plastic Bags	Odds and ends storage
2ea	Labels	Shipping address for taxidermy, etc.
1	Notebook	With pen or pencil to keep a journal or notes
2	Photo Copies	Passport, credit cards, itinerary, emergency contact, customs form 4457
1	Belt ammunition carrier	

1 or 2	pocket ammunition carriers	the kind that do not allow the rounds to clank together

Medical

	Prescriptions	Enough for the trip + 7 days
	Malaria	
	Prophylaxis	As prescribed
	Antibiotic	One course, broad spectrum
	Pain med	Ibuprofen, Tylenol, and Aspirin, etc.
	Decongestants	
	Anti-Diarrheal	
1	Personal 1st Aid Kit	Include Band-Aids, antibiotic ointment, and blister prevention/treatment
1	Insect repellant	(Might be available in camp)
1	Sun Screen	Unscented 30 SPF or better
1	Eye Drops	
1	Lip Balm	
1	Hand Lotion	Unscented
1	Saline Nasal Spray	
1	Tweezers	Briar and splinter removal

Luxury or Extra items

1	Vest	Fleece (warmth) or canvas (thorn protection) lightweight outerwear
1	Bed Shoes	Midnight bathroom breaks and airline comfort
	H20 Flavoring	Individual packs to flavor bottled water.
1pr	Extra Glasses	Prescription glasses or contact lenses
1	Rangefinder	
1	Money Belt	If desired
1	Head net	Mosquito, Mopane fly protection.
1	Wash Cloth	Not always provided

This list should cover just about everything that you could need on a safari. If you are going on a specialized safari, double check with your PH to see if any additional items are required. If you discover anything over the course of your trip that you deem necessary, write it down in your journal. When you get home, transfer it over to your list so that you'll have a reminder for your next trip. This list is just a guideline; feel free to add anything else that you want to take. Just be keep in mind any and all airline restrictions on size or weight.

List of Hints

Hint 1, page 15

When you start investigating the possibility of, or booking, a Safari, get a notebook, and keep it forever.

Keeping all of your notes, thoughts, ideas, records of conversations, and the like, in one place can prove to be invaluable. At the end of the trip, you may want to even consider taking the notebook apart and filing things by category in a divided binder or file for future reference. Just in case, you may want to take another Safari some time.

Hint 2, page 16

Check your prospective booking agents website from time to time to make sure it is updated with new pictures, a price list, and maybe even new camps or locations

A first-class booking agent will have a first-class, up-to-date website.

Hint 3, page 20

Listen to your PH as if your life depended on it because it very well could.

There are all sorts of things in Africa that could stick, sting, scratch, claw, bite, or stomp you. Your PH will get you past these obstacles if you listen to him.

Hint 4, page 23

Always pack a small carry-on bag with what you need to be comfortable if your baggage is lost.

The same goes if you have an unexpected overnight stay without your luggage. Pack what you need, but keep things to a bare minimum.

Hint 5, page 27

Use a travel agency that specializes in African travel for hunters.

This is very important; these folks know of and eliminate problems before you find out that the problems even exist. By using the specialized agency, you will save yourself a lot of wasted time and effort.

Hint 6, page 32

Be ready for anything when you're in Africa, because anything can happen, and it usually does.

What I am really saying here is to be adaptive. The more flexible you are, the more fun and success you will have.

Hint 7, page 34

Plan your carry-on for small planes.

Once you reach your connecting flight in Africa, there is a good chance that it will be on a small plane. You may have to check your carry-on plane-side, even if it is regulation size and ok for a larger plane.

Hint 8, page 35

Never bother your wife with your travel problems if you are going on the trip without her.

Unless you like sleeping in the same location as your hunting dogs, this is not a good idea. 'Nuff said.

Hint 9, page 35

On each leg of your flight, check to make sure that your baggage was transferred.

This might sound like overkill, but, if your baggage was not transferred, it will catch up with you much quicker the earlier the airline knows about it. It is awfully difficult to hunt in Africa without your guns.

Hint 10, page 36

If your flight schedule allows it, get a day room.

Taking a day room and getting out of the airport for a while can do wonders for you in a thirty-plus hour trip. A nap in a bed and a nice hot shower are wonderful things.

Hint 11, page 37

Fill out all declaration and immigration forms before you leave the plane. It will save you time and effort.

Filling them out on the plane will allow you to ask the flight attendants (who speak fluent English) any questions that you may have about filling out the forms. When you hand a customs / immigration official a correctly and completely filled out form, it tends to make their day much better and that may have a direct effect on what type of day you will have.

Hint 12, page 39

If you need a charter fight, do everything possible to try to share the flight and cost with another hunter(s).

This is self-explanatory; charters are very expensive. Share the flight and save some money.

Hint 13, page 39

To help find someone with whom to share the charter flight, with your safari operator to see if they have any other clients flying in and which airport they are using.

Doing this will increase your odds of being able to share a charter flight.

Hint 6a, page 42

Look out for the unexpected. Africa is full of surprises and will spring them on you at any time.

Maybe I should have included this in hint 6, but, to me, there is enough difference for it to warrant its own listing.

Hint 14, page 45

Combine all of what is on the "what to take" list that you receive, remove any duplicate items, and then adjust the list to suit your personal preferences.

If you have never been to Africa before, there are a great many items that you will need that will not even cross your mind until you need them. Studying and combining multiple lists will improve your chances of having everything you need.

Hint 15, page 49

Since most toiletry items like shampoo, body wash, and the like come in large sizes, buy some small bottles and transfer a portion of each item to them. Make sure the bottles are 3 oz. or less so that you can put them in your carry-on bag.

Having these will complete the "what you need to be comfortable" segment in your carry-on bag.

Hint 16, page 49

Save an old prescription bottle for each medication that you take.

Most customs agents do not like loose, unlabeled pills. By having an extra bottle, you can split up your medication to reduce the chance of losing all of it.

Hint 17, page 56

Use more of the smaller-capacity memory cards for your digital cameras, instead of just a few extra large capacity memory cards, or download your cards to a back-up device often.

Although rare, memory cards are not perfect and you can lose your pictures. I know this from personal experience. If a small-capacity card goes bad, you have lost fewer pictures.

Hint 18, page 57

Make two copies of ALL of your paperwork and keep them in separate locations.

If not having it will cause you problems, make copies of it. You will be better off having copies and not needing them than the other way around.

Hint 19, page 58

Re-zeroing your rifle with one shot. Using a bore sight, get as close to zero as possible and then leave the scopes adjustment caps off. Use enough sandbags to get the rifle rock solid steady to allow you to return it to the same position after you fire it. Fire one shot. The shot should be on the paper since you used a bore sight, and make sure you can see the bullet hole somewhere in your scope's field of view. Return the rifle to your original shooting position with the crosshairs on the bull's-eye and use the sandbags to anchor the rifle firmly in this position. While you are looking through the scope have your PH turn the dials on your scope to move the crosshairs to the bullet hole. Your scope is now looking where the bullet hit and is back to zero.

Using this method can save you a lot of ammo if your scope is out of its zero while in Africa. Since you have only a limited amount of ammunition, this is a good thing.

Hint 20, page 63

Bring a rifle that is chambered in a caliber that ammunition is locally available.

If the bag with your ammo is lost, you may be in trouble. If you can buy ammunition while you are in Africa, it can save your hunt.

Hint 21, page 63

If you are traveling with a companion or another hunter, divide up your ammunition among each other's bags.

This will cut down on your chances that you will lose all of your ammunition.

Hint 22, page 73

Unless your PH tells you otherwise, leave your scope on its lowest setting.

Leaving a scope on its lowest setting gives you the greatest field of view and the quickest target acquisition.

Hint 23, page 80

Buy a set of three-legged shooting sticks, and shoot at least two hundred rounds from them.

Shooting from shooting sticks is not difficult, but it is different, and practice makes perfect.

Hint 24, page 80

If you do not already have one, get a scoped .22 rifle with the same action that your Safari rifle has.

This will allow you to practice, frequently and economically.

Hint 25, page 81

Practice getting ready and being able to take a quick follow-up shot.

Do not relax and admire your shot after you take it; your trophy might get up and run off. African game is extraordinarily tough. As soon as you pull the trigger, work the action, keep your quarry in the scope, and be ready to shoot again.

Hint 26, page 81

When you bring a scoped rifle to your shoulder, keep both eyes open and focused on your target, until you see the target through your scope. Then, you can close the other eye.

If you practice doing this, you will get you on target and ready to shoot as fast as possible.

Hint 27, page 89

Let your safari operator know your food preferences, and, more importantly, your food restrictions such as food allergies.

This should keep you happy and healthy at the dinner table.

Hint 28, page 89

Bring an old-fashioned wind-up alarm clock with you. Get yourself up and to breakfast on time.

This will keep someone from having to get up extra early to get you up. It will also keep your PH from waiting on you to have breakfast and get you started hunting on time.

Hint 29, page 90

Take a travel mug with a closable lid with you.

If you like a cup of coffee to go, the travel mug is the only way you will not end up wearing it while you travel over the bumpy ground on your way to your hunting location.

Hint 30, page 90

Take an afternoon nap, if possible.

The better rested you are the better hunt you will have. Besides, everyone else will probably be taking one.

Hint 31, page 94

Do yourself a favor, diet and loose a few pounds before going to Africa, because will probably gain a few while you are there.

Yes, the food really is that good.

Hint 32, page 96

If you like wine with certain dinner choices, check the menu before ordering your choice of cocktail for your sundowner.

Remember the old rhyme about mixing types of alcohol: Liquor on beer (or wine), never fear. Beer on liquor, never sicker.

Hint 33, page 98

Keep a daily journal.

This is very important. If you do not write things down while they are fresh in your mind, the details are lost forever.

Hint 34, page 99

Take all of your gear to breakfast with you. That way, you can leave as soon as breakfast is over.

You paid to hunt, so hunt as much as possible.

Hint 35, page 102

Use time spent walking between stalks to learn from your PH.

Knowledge is a great thing. The more you can do for yourself, the more you are going to get out of the experience.

Hint 36, page 105

Hunt guinea fowl with a .22 rifle.

Hunting guinea this way is some of the most fun I have ever had and I suggest that you give it a shot. (See story in chapter one.)

Hint 37, page 107

The next time a gift-giving reason comes around, ask your spouse for a book.

Start your hunting reference library.

Hint 38, page 108

Even though your PH can tell you when and if to shoot, only you can decide if you should shoot

Do not try shots that are beyond your ability or that you are not comfortable taking.

Hint 39, page 109

Establish an exercise routine, and stick with it.

I know everybody says this, but, to me, everyone saying it just makes it even truer. You will enjoy your hunt more if you are in good physical shape.

Hint 40, page 110

Plan out your trophy photo shoot, write it down, and take the list with you. You should also go over your list with your PH to make sure both of you are on the same page.

If you don't make the list and take it with you, you are liable to forget something when you are caught up in the excitement of the moment. By going over your list with your PH, you are making sure he knows what you want. If he does not know you want something, he does not know to give it to you.

Hint 41, page 111

Wash any blood and dirt off your trophy before you take any pictures.

This just makes for better pictures.

Hint 42, page 113

Bring a small tripod for group or timed-exposure pictures.

This one small light device can save you so much trouble. If you want everyone in the group photograph, you have to have a tripod unless you are able to balance your camera on a rock or something. The night skies in Africa are gorgeous because there is no ambient light. A tripod can give you the ability to capture it in a photograph.

Hint 43, page 118

Visit a local taxidermist before you leave Africa, especially if you are considering having your taxidermy work done there.

There is nothing better that a face-to-face evaluation.

Hint 44, page 120

If it is feasible, ask your PH to take you to visit the taxidermist he uses, and, if it is possible, when he is there checking his mounts, ask, would he please check on yours, as well.

Again, a face-to-face evaluation is best. If your PH will agree to check on your trophy before it is shipped, you could be saving yourself a headache.

Hint 45, page 125

Set your internal clock to "island time".

Things happen at a different pace outside of the United States. If you can adapt your pace to the locality that you are visiting, you can save yourself a great deal of stress.

Hint 46, page 128

Consider yourself a guest in someone else's home.

Even though you are a paying client, consider acting as if you were a guest in someone else's home, because, in reality, you are. Besides that, good manners never killed anyone. If you need to stand up for yourself, by all means, do so, but be polite while doing it.

Below is a copy of the survey that Veldsmans sent me before I went to Africa the first time. I left my answers for illustration purposes and so it would be evident how Johann and Vera Veldsman put them to good use.

Shona Hunting Adventures
Questionnaire

Dear Client,

In order for us to satisfy all your needs while you are hunting with us, we ask that you fill in this questionnaire and return it to us.

Full Name: David Lewis Brown
Age: 46
Occupation: Retired
Religion: Methodist

State of fitness (poor, fair, excellent): Good. I can walk at a steady pace all day. If the grade is steep, I have to slow down but can still keep a slow steady pace. The only times I have problems is over 7000 feet in elevation.

Smoking or non-smoking: Casual smoking.

Medical condition (Allergies, Diabetic, Heart condition, etc.): None

Food preferences: I am a meat & potatoes kind of guy, but I also enjoy fresh fruit & salads. I tend to prefer spicy dishes to bland ones & I love to try local dishes.

Drinking preferences: Soda preferences, Coke & Dr. Pepper, diet Dr. Pepper, & diet Pepsi. One choice is ok -- do not need them all. I tend to like amber to dark beer along the lines of Harp, Newcastle, or Guinness. These are suggestions of style, not specific beers, but either will be great.

I also like to try local beer. As for liquor, a single bottle of a Kentucky bourbon or Canadian blend would be ok. I like ginger ale to mix with. I am not a heavy drinker, so I do not need a huge supply. If wine will be served with dinner, I like dry red table wine with red meat. Otherwise, I will drink soda or beer with dinner.

Is this your first time hunting in Africa? Yes.

If not please state were and tell me a bit about the trophies taken:

Your wish list concerning trophies: While I do not expect a record book animal, I would like a better than average animal. My philosophy about hunting might help you understand my choices a little better. To me the hunt is about the experience not the kill. I would prefer to enjoy the place, companionship & savor the experience & not take an animal than just take a below-average specimen. The best part will be just hunting Africa.

Rifles and caliber you will be hunting with: 300 Weatherby Mag, hand loaded with Barnes 3x shock 180gr @3100 fps. My back up will be an 8x57 Mauser again loaded with 180 gr Barnes 3x. @ 2600 fps. I could also bring a 6.5x55 Mauser with 129gr or 140gr ammo or a 45-70 with 405 gr bullets.

Preferred way of hunting (walk and stalk, ambush, driving, etc.: Whatever works best for the game we are after, but driving game makes me nervous without the proper safeguards in place

What part of the hunt do you enjoy the most? All of it, from the planning to skinning to the eating.

Other hobbies: Target & Skeet shooting, fishing, snow skiing, sailing--
pretty much anything outside.

Anything else you wish to bring under our attention?

Greetings from Africa
Johann and Vera Veldsman

Resources

The following web-links will put you in touch with the people that helped me make my safari an incredible experience:

- Rick Wilks, booking agent; http://www.wilkssafari.com/

- Johann Veldsman, Professional Hunter & Safari Owner; http://www.shona-adventures.com/

- Phillip Smythe, Professional Hunter & Safari Owner; http://www.ivorytrailsafaris.com/

- Sylvia Janbey, Otjwarongo Taxidermy; http://www.namibia-taxidermy.com/index.html

- CZ USA, Safari Classic Rifles; http://www.cz-usa.com/

- Gracy Travel; http://www.gracytravel.com/

- www.safari101book.com

- www.DavidLBrownAuthor.com

BUY A SHARE OF THE FUTURE IN YOUR COMMUNITY

These certificates make great holiday, graduation and birthday gifts that can be personalized with the recipient's name. The cost of one S.H.A.R.E. or one square foot is $54.17. The personalized certificate is suitable for framing and will state the number of shares purchased and the amount of each share, as well as the recipient's name. The home that you participate in "building" will last for many years and will continue to grow in value.

Here is a sample SHARE certificate:

HABITAT FOR HUMANITY

THIS CERTIFIES THAT

__YOUR NAME HERE__

HAS INVESTED IN A HOME FOR A DESERVING FAMILY

1985-2010

TWENTY-FIVE YEARS OF BUILDING FUTURES
IN OUR COMMUNITY ONE HOME AT A TIME

1200 SQUARE FOOT HOUSE @ $65,000 = $54.17 PER SQUARE FOOT
This certificate represents a tax deductible donation. It has no cash value.

YES, I WOULD LIKE TO HELP!

I support the work that Habitat for Humanity does and I want to be part of the excitement! As a donor, I will receive periodic updates on your construction activities but, more importantly, I know my gift will help a family in our community realize the dream of homeownership. **I would like to SHARE in your efforts against substandard housing in my community!** *(Please print below)*

PLEASE SEND ME _____ SHARES at $54.17 EACH = $ $_____

In Honor Of: _____

Occasion: (Circle One)   *HOLIDAY*   *BIRTHDAY*   *ANNIVERSARY*

      OTHER: _____

Address of Recipient: _____

Gift From: _____ *Donor Address:* _____

Donor Email: _____

I AM ENCLOSING A CHECK FOR $ $_____ PAYABLE TO HABITAT FOR HUMANITY OR PLEASE CHARGE MY VISA OR MASTERCARD *(CIRCLE ONE)*

Card Number _____ Expiration Date: _____

Name as it appears on Credit Card _____ Charge Amount $ _____

Signature _____

Billing Address _____

Telephone # Day _____ Eve _____

PLEASE NOTE: Your contribution is tax-deductible to the fullest extent allowed by law.
Habitat for Humanity • P.O. Box 1443 • Newport News, VA 23601 • 757-596-5553
www.HelpHabitatforHumanity.org

CPSIA information can be obtained
at www.ICGtesting.com
Printed in the USA
JSHW040832060422
24632JS00001B/81